Buoyant

Buoyant

How Water and Willpower Helped Wella to Channel
Aaron and Hayley Peirsol

WELLA HARTIG WITH LAURA COTTAM SAJBEL

Red Wheelbarrow Press, Inc. Austin, Texas

ISBN 978-0-9659961-3-6

The cure for anything is salt water—sweat, tears, or the sea.

—ISAK DINESEN

TABLE OF CONTENTS

Little Mermaid

We did not go on a lot of vacations, but we went once to Lake Tahoe with friends of my parents, François and Juliette Van de Voorde and their kids, Ricky, Viviane, and Gui. We stayed in a hotel around the lake. It was the early 1960s, and the hotel was like you'd see in an old movie, with a pool outside. My dad would get in, but he would breaststroke with both feet still on the bottom. My parents, who were from Nova Scotia, didn't know how to swim.

I was six years old. I was holding on to the edge of the pool—testing how it was to be deeper. I remember getting to the rope strung with buoys, like they use to divide the pool. Little did I know there was a deep end.

I had my tummy over the buoy and somehow slipped. I remember sinking, floating, touching the bottom of the pool and not being afraid, a weird sort of calm. At the bottom, I remember the feeling, seeing the bottom of the pool. Blue water all around me, and it was quiet. I noticed white pebbles on the bottom of the pool.

Then Juliette was taking me out, and everyone was screaming and yelling. I was saved; I must have been drowning.

I've always wondered why I wasn't petrified of water. Why wasn't I petrified? All I remember was being calm. When it was all over, I went right back to the pool steps. I loved it too much. I didn't know then I loved the water.

Serendipity: Meeting Wella

ONE PARTICULAR MORNING I FOUND MYSELF—steamed yet again by a disagreement with my twelve-year-old—drawn to my usual lane of the humble neighborhood pool, among my usual friends, who are parents of children several years older than mine.

I fumed about my preteen at the end of our workout, while my friends listened and laughed knowingly, reminding me that this is just one of those layers of hell through which we must pass to earn our ranking as parents of grown-ups.

"Just block off ages thirteen through eighteen," Patricia remarked with a grin. "They're not even civil."

"I'm sorry to eavesdrop," interjected a tanned, wiry newcomer to the bench, stepping out of her sweatpants, "but I have a twenty-five-year-old still at that point." She went on to tell us that she also had a twenty-seven-year-old. After long encouraging her kids to wait until thirty to get married, she frets now because her son doesn't even have a girlfriend. She lamented that parents can never quit worrying.

As it was a sunny, warm March morning in Austin, Texas, we stood exchanging a few more pleasantries on the pool deck in the sun, soaking up the company and the spring weather. Then the interloper stepped to a lane to begin her workout, pulling on a black swim cap, emblazoned with the American flag and, in white capital letters, "PEIRSOL."

The cogs of my brain began to turn. Being a swimmer in a town where some of the world's foremost swimmers train at the University of Texas, in the Lee & Joe Jamail Texas Swim Center, I knew that name. That kind of a cap is printed for members of the U.S. Olympic Team. I looked at this trim and vibrant woman, some five or ten years my senior. Just a fan? Or could it be. . . .

I worked up my nerve as she sat on the edge of the pool adjusting her goggles. "Wait," I ventured, "You wouldn't happen to be the mother of Aaron Peirsol?"

She looked at me, pleased, and smiled. "I am," she confirmed quietly.

* * * *

For those readers not familiar with Aaron Peirsol, think Olympian. Aaron Peirsol, born July 23, 1983, is recognized as one of the greatest backstroke swimmers in history. Over the course of three consecutive Summer Olympic Games in 2000, 2004, and 2008, Aaron won seven medals. Aaron Piersol was on *that* 4x100-meter medley relay in Beijing with Michael Phelps, at the 2008 Olympics, the event where Phelps won his history-making eighth gold medal.

So, on a morning that started out with a volcanic argument over whether two middle-school parties may be attended in one evening, I had wound up at the pool with a mother who managed to raise an incredible kid, one who must have exceeded everyone's wildest hopes for him. A kid who had to be dedicated, persevering, and willing to put in the pro-verbial elbow grease. How on earth did his mother make him turn in his middle-school homework and come in before curfew, much less train enough hours to become world-class in his sport? At our familiar, unimpos-ing Stacy Pool, built by the Works Progress Administration on the back of the Great Depression, I felt I'd had a brush with greatness.

In turning to go, I had to say something. It was heartfelt. I managed to whisper, "All of us with twelve-year-olds kneel before you."

And then I found out there was more.

—Laura Cottam Sajbel

Chapter 1 : Perspective

Wella's Tip for Staying Afloat: *Be there to share that moment. If you can, touch their skin or look in their eyes when they break a record. You've gone where no one else has gone.*

AT THE START OF AN OLYMPIC RACE, the adrenaline courses through your veins and your heart pounds. Thousands watch from a crowded arena and millions more peer through the telephoto lens that is beaming your beads of sweat to the world. The Olympic pool stretches before you, a sparkling aquamarine, and the familiar scent of chlorine permeates the air. A swimmer one lane over shakes his arms to loosen up, setting in motion a powerful ripple along his body. Anticipating the start signal, every muscle tenses, coiled to spring.

Five-time gold medalist Aaron Peirsol claims that you can shut all that out, that reaching the Olympics is *almost* anticlimactic, after the insanely competitive Olympic Trials. He will tell you that elite contestants at the start of an Olympic race concentrate single-mindedly on what it will take to win. Maybe that kind of mind control is exactly what has allowed him to power through twenty years of racing while making it all look elegant and effortless.

After a young lifetime spent in training to reach the Olympics, how thrilled yet perhaps vulnerable an individual athlete must feel at the pinnacle of sports. Those who make it to this rarefied peak are few; those who triumph even fewer. And in the wake of each swimmer, runner, or gymnast churns a story of how that athlete arrived at this moment, a history of genetics and circumstances and paths taken.

Like the storied gods of Olympus, modern Olympians and their families can be noble and stoic, jealous and competitive, with an inexplicably intense drive. Studies prove that elite athletes are born with genetic advantages—measurably higher ratios of fast- or slow-twitch muscles; preternaturally high levels of red blood cells to carry oxygen and a metabolism geared to process that excess oxygen; body structures perfectly suited to their sport. However, there are also intangibles—equally weighted—that beg to be more thoroughly explored. Where do athletes get the will and the psychological stamina to train to the limits of human capacity and to withstand the scrutiny of the media and the public, both of which are second-guessing every breath and watching for a spectacular downfall? Ancient gods were carved of marble to last for eternity. What is it, precisely, that chisels the physiques and hones the unflinching determination of elite human athletes?

It should come as no surprise that every successful athlete requires a support crew, someone who nurtured, bandaged, fed, and drove to practice the young phenom. In the case of the Peirsol siblings, Aaron and his athletic sister Hayley (also an Olympic contender and world-ranked swimmer), that support has been primarily their mother, Wella, a spunky woman who had dreams of greatness for her children.

Parenting is hardly less daunting than being an elite athlete perched at the start of a race: A baby's very life depends on its parents' choices and circumstances. Though we are sent home with registration papers and troubleshooting guides for products as inconsequential as a new toaster, there is no handbook to rear any child, let alone one born with a magnificent and undeniable talent. While many parents of gifted athletes may navigate some of the same waters, potential alliances between them are often cut off in the swirl of envy and rivalry that becomes ever more fierce, the more talented a child might be.

Finding all the traits necessary for great athletic accomplishment combined in one individual is extraordinary. Even more exceptional is the person who is not only a great athlete but is considered a fine human being. Add longevity to this torchbearer's career and a sibling with similar talents, and you have the makings of an amazing tale. What on earth did their mother feed those kids?

The twist is that it's not just about what Wella has been feeding Aaron and Hayley; it's about the environment she created for them. By doing for them what she found necessary for herself, she channeled their energy into athletics. Their story is not just about sports; it's about finding balance.

* * *

WELLA RAISED AARON AND HAYLEY PEIRSOL in and around Irvine, California, a master-planned community that sprouted during the housing boom of the 1960s. Stucco houses in Irvine are coated in earth tones and grouped into villages, each surrounded by orderly stucco walls. Nearly fifty miles of wide, concrete pathways meander among the various villages with studied nonchalance, set back from the streets in lush green, neatly trimmed grass, connecting neighborhood parks, greenbelts, and nature preserves.[1]

The streets around Irvine are expansive and impeccably manicured, tidily lined with trees planted in perfect rows. On some streets, those trees are extraordinarily tall Torrey pines; elsewhere are meticulously groomed palms, their naked trunks reaching up to a headdress of fringed fronds. Pungent eucalyptus are the signature trees, their ivory trunks carefully shaved of the ubiquitous peeling bark, their menthol aroma lending a scent of the exotic. With the ocean only a couple of miles down the road, the air is infused with a sea-breeze softness and muted light. The attractive sand beaches and the Mediterranean climate issue an open invitation—maybe even a siren song—to live outdoors.

Corona del Mar, from Inspiration Point on the southern edge. The further spit of land in the distance is The Wedge, a spot known for its dangerous surf.
PHOTO: LAURA COTTAM SAJBEL

Nearby, the towns of Costa Mesa, Newport Beach, and Corona del Mar extend to the ocean, the playground on which the Peirsol children grew up. They raced across the jewel of a beach that is Corona del Mar, where cement fire rings, bench-level walls, elegant carved trash cans, and blue beach umbrellas give the public park the ambience of a private club.

Beginning their official swim careers at an unassuming brown brick YMCA on University Avenue in Newport Beach, the Peirsol siblings proved their determination, stamina, and resilience early on. Once they started training at a more competitive club in Irvine, they rose to the top quickly in the age groups and eventually earned college scholarships at respected universities.

Hayley Peirsol is an athletic demi-goddess in her own right, a long-course record-holder who won two individual and three team NCAA championships with swimming powerhouse Auburn University. Training at Auburn with Ralph Crocker, and with esteemed distance coach Jon Urbanchek and his successor, Bob Bowman, in Michigan, Hayley leaped to prominence in 2003, with world-class times in the 800-meter and 1500-meter freestyle events. She holds the record as the third woman in the world to break the sixteen-minute mark in the 1500-meter freestyle, following Janet Evans and Kate Ziegler. After winning NCAA championships and competing at the US Olympic Trials, Hayley refocused her laser determination on a new sport: triathlon. In tribute to the second incarnation of her sports career, the November 2009 issue of *USA Triathlon*[2] featured her on its cover as Rookie of the Year. On top of her daunting physical prowess, Hayley is known for her animated personality, captivating friends with her own brand of verve.

Aaron Peirsol, the three-time Olympian, embodies a young Neptune with surfer-dude style. Widely regarded as the world's pre-eminent backstroker, he stands six foot three inches, with emerald eyes, curly hair, and an amicable personality. Despite his laid-back persona, he holds individual world records (the best global performances ever recorded and verified)[3] in the 100-meter and 200-meter backstroke events as well as five gold and two silver Olympic medals from three consecutive Games—and has quietly lent his clout to ocean conservation as well as many other charity fundraising efforts.

Aaron was world-ranked in swimming by the age of fifteen, something "virtually unheard of," according to his celebrated coach, Eddie Reese, who first met Aaron at the Olympics and later coached him through college and beyond.[4] Aaron's spectacular career had spanned nearly twenty years at the time of his official retirement from the sport in February 2011. Even more—and more importantly to his mother Wella—is that by all accounts, Aaron is a really nice guy.

Every bit as remarkable as their sports accomplishments are the circumstances that led the family to this point. Wella, who grew up in a household where alcohol and depression impacted the lives of a generation, struggled with hyperactivity and anxiety from the time she was small. When she began running and swimming as a young adult, she discovered for herself the healing power of intense physical effort. She may not have understood it at the time, but that exercise had the power to alter her brain chemistry. She just knew she felt better. When Wella had children of her own, her instinct to put them in the pool helped her raise extremely athletic and energetic kids who, ultimately, set records and won Olympic medals.

Although we're only now unearthing the particulars of how our wonderfully complex biological circuitry works, current studies prove that exercise unleashes the growth of new cells in our brains and plays a crucial role in the body's natural pain control. New scientific evidence suggests that, besides the physical benefits, exercise has the potential to significantly alter mood and harness mental focus. In addition, recent theories divulge ways genius can be cultivated with deliberate practice. For the Peirsol family, it was the perfect storm.

All of us, not just those predisposed to push our bodies to the limits, can learn from Wella's story. She had a rough, disconnected start. But she found a way to turn things around, to channel her energy and turn the tide on her circumstances. We may not all become world-record holders, but we can all find balance in our lives that will make us healthier and better adjusted. More than that, we can accept the circumstances and biology we are given and find the willpower to give our lives meaning and direction.

Wella has managed, despite some serious mistakes, to instill values and compassion in her children. She talks about perspective and generosity of spirit. She talks about seeing others as equals. In her words, "You have to take responsibility for what you raise. You have to raise a person, not just a swimmer." Wella turned dysfunction into greatness, with tenacity and the good fortune of discovering the power of physical exertion to heal.

Chapter 2 : Endurance

Wella's Tip for Staying Afloat: *If you don't dream for your children, there is no one else who's going to dream for them.*

CLEAR FROM THE START IS THAT WELLA KNOWS how to make an impression. She arrives at an initial interview well-appointed in a tailored turquoise-and-white sheath dress, hair coiffed, coffee in hand (The Coffee Bean's "Black Forest Ice-Blended" with whipped cream and a cherry, her usual lunch). Despite her polished appearance, she exudes a childlike quality, with round, ice-blue eyes; that distinctive, husky voice reminiscent of your favorite high-school cheerleader; and a sensitive nature, inspiring those who love her to indulge and protect her. Driving a white Mercedes station wagon and sporting a short, sun-bleached haircut, Wella looks like a product of upscale Southern California, which isn't far from the truth. Nearly five foot seven and *almost* 110 pounds, she is slim, athletic—in amazing shape for her fifty-something years—full of energy, and eager to chat.

Wella's tale, though true, reads like a soap opera—family rivalry, unrequited love, glamorous settings, heroes and villains, a brush with the law, and a brush with the gods. What really sets her apart is that, through a period as a single parent and many financial and emotional setbacks, she has mothered two remarkable athletes. For her to recognize early on how to channel Aaron's and Hayley's energies and talents was part luck and part resolve.

"If you have one of those kids, you just *know* it," Wella quips, in her typical animated fashion, referring to the type of child who begins jumping out of the crib at four months and never stops moving. Lightning may not strike twice, but in the case of the Peirsol kids, it came awful close.

Wella wasn't exactly blessed with a set of instructions for how to raise children. She grew up feeling set adrift by parents who didn't seem to have the capacity for the kind of unconditional love Wella craved, a dynamic that reverberated throughout the lives of the family members. The longing for stability and approval left its mark. Her siblings, who married successful spouses or pursued lucrative careers, appear to have gravitated toward the acceptance and prestige that follow material success.

Wella's emotional emptiness drove her to look elsewhere to fill that void, which set her on a completely different path. She dreamed of turning all that hurt around by treating children of her own with love and giving them firm direction.

* * *

THE LOLLING, DUSTY SANTA ANA MOUNTAINS repose like a line of wrinkled elephants on the horizon, haze blurring them in the distance. The sky is a glaring white and the atmosphere hints at proximity to the coast, as the tinge of salty sea air mingles with the metallic taste of metropolitan pollution from the surrounding freeways. Back in the 1950s and '60s, this part of California was largely rural. The charming town square of Orange, California, near the house where Wella grew up, looks like an idyllic place to raise a family.

Margaret and Joseph Morrison had moved with their three children from Nova Scotia to sunny Southern California in 1956, ostensibly for the sake of Margaret's health. They must have had a little money saved from their sundries store in Sydney, Nova Scotia, because they purchased ten acres of orange groves. Joseph, who was in construction, built the family a big, white modern ranch house with a flat roof, right in the middle of their land. The Sunkist company[5] came to buy their oranges.

The family returned to Nova Scotia for a visit the summer after their move. While they were there, on August 18, 1957, their fourth child was born. They named their newest daughter after a nun on duty in the hospital, Mary Louella.

Louella remembers hearing how her brother Joey had been sent to live with their paternal grandparents when she was a baby. It wasn't until she was in her fifties, recounting the story of her birth, that she suddenly realized her parents must have left Joey in Nova Scotia on that trip, after she was born. She had always heard that her grandparents took care of Joey because he was only a year and a half when she came along, and that it was too much for her mother, Margaret, to care for two small children as well as the older girls,

Barbara and Patte.

When Louella herself was a year and a half old, Joey rejoined the family in California, and a jealous rivalry developed that has shadowed their relationship throughout their lives. In one example of sibling tension, Joey took Louella, who was barely walking, on a stroll into the orchards and returned without her. He passed off her absence as no fault of his. He didn't know where she could have gone. The fire department and the family went looking and found her at the bottom of a dry well, in the company of a dead possum, surrounded by broken glass. A white scar, where a cut had to be stitched after that incident, still streaks her tanned calf. Little Louella was lucky: The next day, as the story goes, that well refilled. The family would recall the tale, laughing and teasing that Joey pushed her, something he always denied.

When the hot, dry Santa Ana winds began to gust down from the mountains east of Orange County each fall, they carried desert sand and fanned wildfire smoke into the shallow coastal valley. Shuttled by the winds, little Louella's graded papers worked their way out of the bushes, where she had crumpled and hidden them on the way home from school, and blew down the street like fallen leaves into the Morrisons' yard, where her mother found them anyway.

Louella started kindergarten at St. Cecilia Catholic School. Her first taste of trouble there came when the nuns repeatedly called roll for "Mary Morrison." Never having heard herself called Mary, Louella didn't respond. When the nuns confronted her, she insisted, "I'm Louella." The nuns then called her older sister in from another class to settle the discrepancy.

"Yes, that is Mary Louella Morrison," Patte confirmed.

"My first name is Mary?" Louella cried in dismay. "Mary Louella?" No one had ever bothered to explain her full name, at least as far as she remembers.

She was annoyed by her long, curly locks and begged her parents to let her get a haircut like a boy. She even begged her brother's barber. Finally, her parents gave in. Louella was thrilled.

"Needless to say, I was not the most popular girl in grammar school," she says now, with a lighthearted but derisive laugh. "I had a short haircut when no one else did. And I always wore shorts under my dresses."

She also hung on the bars until she had to wear Band-Aids on the back of her knees. She spent so much time upside down on the playground that everyone could see under her dress. So, besides the shorts, her mother bought her cotton undershirts to wear with her outfits.

School didn't hold much appeal for Louella, who was diagnosed early on as hyperactive, a diagnosis later revised to attention-deficit hyperactivity disorder, or ADHD. She never liked the medicines she was prescribed because they made her feel drowsy, though she admits she was an overactive, restless child. Even at the tender age of five, Wella (as her family began to call her) fretted more than the average kindergartner about impressing her parents and knew she could not compete on the academic playing field against her older siblings. However, she was a natural athlete with a penchant for daring.

A highlight of Wella's childhood, one that still thrills her when she remembers it, was her bike. Being a fourth child, she got lots of hand-me-downs, including some Barbies. She preferred to play with the dolls after popping off their heads or cutting their hair. In that time period, and in their family, gifts were small at holidays and birthdays. One year for Christmas, though, her parents gave Wella a brand-new bicycle. A gold Stingray with a banana seat, it was a boy's bike, a fact which did not escape notice.

"I can remember other little girls saying, 'It's a boy's bike!' and I'd say, 'Yeah! Isn't it *great*!?' Now I look back and really laugh," Wella declares, grinning, her voice cracking with glee. "I just thought it was *the best*. I loved flying down the street. I'd get some speed going to stand on the banana seat."

Young Wella spent her after-school hours riding her beloved bike wildly through her neighborhood and playing hide-and-seek with the other kids until they had to go in at dark. It's easy to visualize this attractive, energetic woman as a girl, wavy hair platinum from the California sun, skin glowing from days at the beach. As she grew older, she loved dancing to the records of Diana Ross and Michael Jackson, and, in particular, the 5th Dimension's version of "Wedding Bell Blues." In many ways, she claims, she was a typical child of the 1960s.

Margaret Morrison had eventually convinced her husband to leave their spacious orange-grove home and move to a house in Tustin, near Irvine, California, purportedly so her growing kids could ride their bikes in the cul-de-sac with other children. Up to that point, they had had few neighbors, and the ones they had were older. Wella guesses in hindsight that her mother might have been lonely out there in the orange groves. She remembers her mother taking to her bed for days at a time. When she was small, Wella would bring her mother toast, trying to make her feel better. "I think she was probably depressed," Wella says sympathetically.

Wella's parents came from a hard life, she acknowledges.

"I really don't know what molded my mother," Wella reflects. Margaret grew up without her father, who had passed away when she was a child. She went to work very young at a jewelry store and married at what was considered a late age, twenty-seven. Margaret gave birth to Barbara at twenty-eight and had her last baby, Wella, at thirty-eight.

"We were told they moved to California because of mom's bad health. But she never spoke to her brothers," Wella explains. "I think, now, she wanted to get away."

Wella's father, Joseph, had flown bombers in the Royal Canadian Air Force. He had been stationed in Iceland and in London, flying with the Aussies and the Brits. In later years, he would talk about the parts of World War II that weren't so bad. It was generally acknowledged, though unspoken, that he had killed people during the fighting.

"I think the war was something he had to live with the rest of his life," Wella concedes, "and maybe that escalated the drinking, so he wouldn't have to think so much." Aching to spend time with her father, little Wella often pestered him to let her drink a beer, and he would pour some in a cup and let her sit with him.

Joseph and Margaret took the family to church every Sunday. The older girls attended Catholic schools, and Wella attended catechism classes—"the whole nine yards." She reflects now, "When I think back, there was a lot of hypocrisy, in the way I heard people talk badly about each other. Instead, I think you should teach that everyone's the same… and to look for the good."

But always, the house was clean. "At our house, *cleanliness* was close to godliness," Wella says. "Mumma kept an immaculate house and made us to be that way, to an uncomfortable extent." This training seems to have stuck with her. At several junctures later in her life, Wella purged everything as she moved on, and her personal spaces are remarkably and intentionally clean and spare, uncluttered by memorabilia. Growing up in the tidy little hamlet of Orange, and then later living in Irvine, Wella may have subconsciously related to the orderly environment of the mid-century master-planned community.

Her mother focused her energies on being the consummate housewife. Wella recalls dining on lots of food characteristic of the 1960s: Hamburger Helper, Jell-O, and Hawaiian pork chops that came with a pineapple "surprise."

"TV dinners," Wella muses, grinning mischievously. "We really looked forward to TV dinners on Friday night. Foil over the potatoes, chicken and, boy, you really looked forward to that dessert, some sort of apple-crap dessert.… "

The adults in Wella's life were more distant from their four youngsters than is popular among child-rearing experts today. In her experience, fathers came home from the office to their drinks and papers and weren't expected to take a high degree of interest in the daily tribulations of their children. The Morrisons perhaps still believed that children were to be "seen but not heard."

Wella *longed* for more closeness. She was a tomboy who may have seemed carefree and tough, but she craved love and affection from parents who were disposed—perhaps by culture, perhaps by nature—not to be forthcoming with that kind of emotion.

Wella says that things that look dysfunctional in retrospect seemed normal to her then. Expectations may have been different in those days. Generally, there was less parental supervision, less of the hyper-attentive parenting and micromanagement of children that has cropped up in more recent generations. Spankings were a fact of family life. And society was just on the cusp of offering outdoor sports to girls. Perhaps it was a combination of factors. To Wella, her parents' detachment from her personal development felt like emotional abandonment.

"One time," she recalls sadly, "Dad took Joey and me to a park for an Easter egg hunt. It was at a school, with nearby swings and a slide. He dropped us off, but it was the wrong date. We were there, alone, for eight or nine hours. He came and got us at dusk. I remember his big truck rumbling up, and I remember thinking, *He's here! He's here!* We had been there all day without any snacks or drinks. Mother's response was something along the lines of 'Well, we'll just have dinner.'"

After Wella's oldest sister left home for college, the Morrisons upgraded to an even nicer home. However, Joseph Morrison's construction business suffered during a housing slump. They sold their spacious house and moved to a condominium complex called Green Valley, in the town of Fountain Valley, California. Although the downsizing must have been a blow to the family, Wella loved that the condos had an adjacent greenbelt and a community pool where there was a swim team in the summer. That swim team was a major turning point for her. Though she had never learned properly, she watched the other kids and figured out how to swim.

"The coach gave me a basic idea of how to do the strokes. I was nine or ten—very late to get started. But I loved it, just *loved it!* As soon as I got a taste of it, I took off. I flourished. I was falling in love with swimming, in a different sort of way," Wella says, then pauses reflectively. "Maybe I fell in love with the water, instead of with swimming. That was my home."

The coach, Larry Capune, had a big influence on her. A legend in the sport of paddleboarding, Capune had soloed along the California coastline from San Francisco to Newport Beach (542 miles in eighteen days) in 1964.[6] By the time he coached Wella and the Fountain Valley team, he was beginning to draw national attention—and he was surely the heartthrob of any pre-teen girl on the pool deck. He was the quintessential blond, sun-tanned lifeguard—"extremely handsome," Wella declares, tilting her head forward conspiratorially—with a talent for motivational speaking and an oversized craving for adventure.

Perhaps it was Coach Capune who instilled in Wella her admiration of swimmers. Certainly, athletic, adventuresome Wella identified with her coach's risky escapades and engaging personality: This was her first brush with an aquatic hero.

Besides swimming, Wella hung out at the condo's recreational facilities to see movies at the pool on Saturday nights and to play ping-pong.

"I got proficient at ping-pong," she recalls with a lilt of bravado, "and was a *huckster*. I could beat older people. I was meant to be into activities but wasn't put into organized activities. Luckily, I found them myself, or I could have run *amok*."

The summer after fifth grade, when Louella was eleven, the family moved again, to a nice house in Huntington Beach, where she attended Gisler Middle School and, later, Edison High. During those years, Wella admits she "wasn't real academic. I just glided through high school. I don't think I ever studied, and if I did, it was cram-study." Looking back, she regrets that her parents didn't put her in sports, where she is certain she would have thrived. "That would have been my saving grace in school, for sure," she insists.

Her parents did sign her up for ballet, and she adored the outfits but "couldn't be bothered to pay attention to all the details."[7] Tap dance was fun, but she was "too wild" for the discipline. So she eventually wound up performing modern jazz. As she remembers it, though, her parents only came to one dance recital.

"I just didn't expect much because I didn't have anything to compare it to," she summarizes.

For some reason, her sister Patte was "lucky enough" to get diving lessons with US Olympic Hall of Fame diver (and medical doctor) Sammy Lee—providing Wella her second brush with a famous aquatic athlete. Lee had been the first Asian-American to win Olympic gold for the United States, in both 1948 and 1952, and the first man to win back-to-back gold in Olympic platform diving. He later coached Olympic divers Pat McCormick, Bob Webster, and Greg Louganis.[8] Even so, Wella doesn't recall the family ever going to watch Patte dive. She only remembers going to pick her up after practice.

Early on, Wella thought about how she wished her parents had done things, which played out in her deliberate parenting choices when she became a mother. She remembers being spanked at the ages of seven or eight. Much later, when her own children were that age, she would take a very different approach: "I never, ever hit my children because that affected me a lot. In my brain, it was so *distressing*. The person who should love you most is hurting you. It made no sense."

She also refrains from drinking, having watched her father drink so much. "I was determined that wouldn't be me," she insists. "I didn't want to be like that."

However, she does concede that her father "had a different heart than my mother," referring to his sentimental side. "My mom I never saw cry." Her father read poetry—he read *anything*, a fact that may have influenced Wella to pick up biographies when she was older. He would take his book outside to read. Meanwhile, Margaret would scrub the floors on hands and knees—a practice she continued into her eighties—then pop up to go vacuum. She had a lot of energy to apply to her platitudes about cleanliness.

"These are the blocks that built this kid," says Wella. The drive she began to feel to do things differently with her children—to treat them differently and to see them succeed—may have been born of the same competitive tendency that her siblings funneled into prestigious achievements. She just tweaked her tactics and her focus.

In spite of the odds she felt were stacked against her, she developed a tenacity that served her well as she endured uncomfortable circumstances and intense workouts down the line. She also began to imagine enduring values and goals for a family of her own; and, ultimately, she would pass along to her children some of her capacity for fortitude and determination that allowed them to succeed. Because she didn't feel she got hugs and love from her family growing up, she resolved to change that around, too.

"The first thing Aaron does," Wella says now, "he bends down and kisses and hugs me. That's just the way I raised my children. I would be shocked if Aaron didn't do that. He knows how much I love them."

Chapter 3 : Equilibrium

Wella's Tip for Staying Afloat: *If you're given everything, you lose the drive.*

LIKE MANY TEENS, WELLA DIDN'T HAVE A CLEAR DIRECTION after high school. Her friend's father had a connection at Colby-Sawyer College in New Hampshire, someone willing to offer Wella a dance scholarship. Colby was a women's college, with a strong dance program. The brochures made it look quaint and cozy, with red brick buildings abutted by colorful autumn trees. But in the end, there was no beach, and Wella couldn't imagine being so cold in all that snow. She had spent her free time in high school slathering on baby oil and sunning on the beach with her friends. Orange Coast College (OCC) was an easy choice, as nearly "everyone" from Huntington Beach went there after high school. She could still hang out at the beach with her friends and nothing would change much.

At OCC, Wella took basic curriculum, some dance classes, some art. By her own admission, she "loafed and floated." Looking back, she shakes her head about her eighteen-year-old self who gave up so easily on finding her place in the world.

"If I'd had some guidance . . ." She trails off, wistfully. "I didn't have someone to grab hold of me. That's something I did completely different with my kids."

However, two factors at OCC hijacked the meandering course of her life: one particular person and a fitness class.

Wella's best friend introduced her to Scott Peirsol, who had noticed Wella. From Florida, Scott was dark-haired, clean-cut, muscular—a surfer, but unlike any of the shaggy, blond California surfers Wella knew. He wore seersucker pants or plaid Bermuda shorts with thong sandals and Lacoste shirts in pastel colors. Scott's father, Fred Peirsol, had been an All-American swimmer at Cornell (1950–1954) and captain of the swim team there. Scott's mother, Bena Boltin (Bebe) Wells, had been a synchronized swimmer and musician who studied voice and piano at Brenau College in Georgia.[9] Bebe seems to have been ahead of her time in women's athletics, evidenced by old yearbook pages listing her as president of the Recreation Association and active in "Class Sports," including three years in the "Acquacade [sic]."

Wella thought Scott was adorable; that he was a surfer didn't hurt. When she met Scott at age nineteen, she fell head over heels "way too quickly" and within three or four months thought she was ready to get married. Her parents insisted she wait until she turned twenty-one for a wedding, so she and Scott continued their relationship and their college classes, and tied the knot the day after Wella's twenty-first birthday, on August 19, 1978.

Wella's parents distrusted Scott. Though to her Scott appeared thoroughly charming and "everybody loved him," her parents were wary. "My dad sensed early on that Scott was not a worker bee," Wella admits. "His dad was an attorney, so Scott was given a car and everything he wanted. He expected to look wealthy, but he didn't really want to go out and work. He felt entitled."

Scott worked for a while for Wella's dad, but that didn't last too long. "Scott would quit a job, but then he always found another one," Wella explains. "That just doesn't work when you have a family." He worked on boats and in other capacities that involved living on yachts for a while, sometimes skippering vessels from one location to another, so the couple stored many of their belongings at her parents' home. Each gig ended rather abruptly, she recalls. Wella stuck by him. "Why? I have no clue," she says now, "except I thought he'd get better."

Before Wella even realized what was causing the friction, her frustration with some of Scott's traits began to eat at their relationship. For a long while, she tried to brush off her insecurities about him. She and Scott lived in Laguna Beach, where it seemed that everyone ran. So Wella began running, at first barefoot on the beach. Later, she bought running shoes and ran along the Pacific Coast Highway.

"I was young and had something to prove," she observes. One of her regular routes was the stretch of beach from Laguna to Corona del Mar, a round trip of nearly twelve miles. Those intense runs became her equilibrium, helping her put her troubles in perspective and concentrate on the positive. And in the running, she rediscovered some of that freedom and happiness she'd found in childhood while riding her bike recklessly through the neighborhood. Neuroscientists now understand how that level of intense exercise would have been sufficient to lift her mood, sharpen her mental

Flowers drape the Goldenrod Footbridge, which connects the downtown to houses just above Corona del Mar beach, where Scott and Wella rented.
PHOTO: LAURA COTTAM SAJBEL.

focus, and release stress.[10] Wella had inadvertently discovered the healthiest possible prescription for her worries. Instinctively, she began cultivating a means of coping that would profoundly shape her life and, later, the lives of her children.

Things for the young couple looked rosy on the surface. After Laguna, the Peirsols rented a succession of airy modern houses a block from the ocean in Corona del Mar, on a street draped with magenta, coral, and lavender blossoms. Two of the houses she and Scott rented were located just west of the cute shops downtown, near the historic Goldenrod Footbridge, built across a steep ravine in the 1920s to connect residents more easily to the beach. To make extra money, Wella printed up some business cards and started her own small business tending plants for local offices. At each of the rented homes where they had a yard, Wella left another type of calling card, too: She always planted roses.[11]

The wide sidewalks and beach lent themselves easily to running. Even now, years later, on a recent crisp fall morning, everyone in sight wears matched athletic attire, and the palm tree–lined sidewalks are peppered with neighbors out for their morning run.

Around this time, Wella, perhaps influenced by her father's penchant for literature, began to read books that would prove formative for her. She read James Fixx's popular *The Complete Book of Running*, published in 1977, a book that helped instigate the national revolution in running for exercise. When Quaker Oats sponsored a 10K race in Griffith Park in Los Angeles, Wella got James Fixx to sign her copy of his book as well as a Quaker Oats box. She remembers him as the reason she started reading about running. Later she picked up *Marathon Mom: The Wife and Mother Running Book,* by Linda Schreiber. That book, published in 1980, before Wella even had kids, inspired her to run regardless of her circumstances.

"The author talked about running in her driveway when she couldn't leave her twins," Wella remembers. The books encouraged her to run and stick with it, which helped Wella begin to focus herself and her energy.

On a whim, she got the idea that she should try out for the OCC track team. The coach happened to be the same person who had coached track at Wella's high school. Although he never discouraged her, she recognized right away that running on her own hadn't put her in league with the other women who had been training for track. Nonetheless, the coach not only allowed Wella to run with the cross-country team, he also introduced the idea of cross-training and suggested she try the swim-for-fitness class offered at OCC—"the greatest advice that guy gave me," she affirms.

Though her only experience with swimming had been the summer team back in Fountain Valley, Wella signed up for the swim-for-fitness class. At first, she didn't even know how to wear goggles without getting leaks. The swim coach at OCC, Ted Bandaruk, instructed the class to swim for thirty minutes, and Wella remembers freezing in the water. At first, the other side of the pool looked so far away, and she worried, "I'm going to be swimming lengths back and forth in this?"

Fortunately, her tenacity kicked in. She set her sights on swimming a mile and worked toward that goal. "The class would be gone, and I didn't have another class afterward, so I'd do a mile every day—and run. And that's what I've done pretty much ever since," she states matter-of-factly, of a regimen that many people would find daunting. Among the students, she recognized one guy who had been on the swim team at her high school and asked him, "What makes somebody fast?" Looking back, Wella laughs. "Now I can't believe I bothered him in the middle of his set, but he said something that stayed with me: 'Think about being as long as you possibly can be in the water, like somebody's pulling you on a string.'

"Swimming was so exhilarating and so freeing. You had nobody yelling in your ear. I wasn't being coached, really. Given the right coaching, I could have been good. But it was a no-brainer to love it. It's the most natural thing in the world to me. I like the feel of the water," she explains.

"It is a necessity, not just an escape," Wella says, trying to put her finger on exactly what she means. "I had to do something physical. Running is freeing, too. The two combined—the most amazing ever."

With the intensity of her workouts notched up, Wella noticed she could think more clearly and calmly, and she felt more relaxed.

"So I was lucky to find swimming and running to love. It made me euphoric when I got out of the pool. Later, it made me a happier and better mom. It became my way of de-stressing, even before I had children. I already had it fixed in my head.

"Sometimes I get emotional: What if I'd had parents that directed me?" she asks. "I'm kind of sad because I could have been an athlete. But I didn't burn out on running and swimming. Probably if I'd started earlier . . ." She trails off, then reframes her point.

"I'm lucky to have two knees that still run. Really, I love what I do. If things had worked out differently, I don't know if I'd have had Hayley and Aaron."

She had stumbled into exercise and found something fulfilling—even if her runs and swims took on the look of obsession. Discovering that intense exercise bolstered her sense of well-being, Wella began a daily regimen that incorporated rising by 5:00 or 6:00 a.m. for a long run, plus a mile swim. Right around that time, the sport of triathlon was taking root in nearby Mission Bay, California, though that craze didn't catch Wella's eye. Coincidentally, during these years, the nascent experiments of a group of neuroscientists began to show the effects of exercise on mood disorders.

Intense, regular exercise summoned for Wella the inner resources to direct her energy in a positive way and began to develop in her a stronger, more confident outlook. Having her children to love and tend to added another rich dimension, giving her a clearer direction and focus for her life.

When Wella first found out she was pregnant, the doctor said she could continue doing whatever activities she usually did. He must not have recognized exactly whom he was addressing. At five foot six and three-quarters of an inch, she weighed about 105 pounds and was running ten to twelve miles and swimming for an hour every day. She remembers carrying both babies so low that she had to lift up her belly while she ran. Finally, when pregnancy started affecting her sciatic nerve, she had to reduce her miles to seven or eight on the runs, but swimming felt great. "I don't care what anyone says," she says, "I believe if you swim when you're pregnant, it helps with your delivery."

Intriguingly, scientific studies now prove that atrial natriuretic peptide (ANP), a hormone produced in the heart and in the brain, naturally counteracts stress and blunts anxiety. Levels of this hormone are ramped up during pregnancy, a biological strategy to protect the developing baby's brain from the stress and anxiety of the mother. Aerobic exercise also amplifies the amount of ANP in the body, causing a notable lessening of anxiety and panic.[12] In more ways than one, Wella was doing her best to give Aaron and Hayley the best possible start in life.

While she swam, Wella daydreamed about the children she would have someday. "Truly, I wanted my kids to be swimmers—even when they were in utero. So I would swim and have plenty of time to daydream. Their father was dark-skinned, with dark eyes. Though Aaron came out blond and green-eyed, completely different from what I imagined, I dreamed that my son or daughter was going to be a swimmer. I just had this feeling of 'I can't wait!'"

Aaron was born in 1983 in Orange, arriving at a hefty eight pounds, eight ounces. Hayley came along in 1985 in Newport Beach, weighing seven pounds, eleven ounces. "My kids were Gerber babies," Wella recalls fondly. "They were big and round and healthy. Both could swim before they could walk." They were athletic kids from the start, better balanced, stronger, and especially in Hayley's case, much harder to keep up with than the other children Wella saw around her.

Luckily, as she took on the responsibilities of motherhood, she had her release valve already in place: "I ran with Aaron in a Peg Perego [stroller]. I wore out the wheels. I got a new navy one for Hayley, and a double for both of them, and ran the hills around Corona del Mar. That was rare at the time. People would call out, 'Where's the fire?'"

And she still swam. "For me, at each point in my life the water has been different. In the beginning, it was an adventure," she muses. "When the kids were little it was an escape. A sitter would watch Aaron for an hour, when he was a baby, and there was a pool at Promontory Point[13] with gorgeous Balboa Island views where I could swim. It was time to get away from the baby."

Later, she would bring little Aaron to the pool, packing along a playpen for him while she did her laps.

"He was gorgeous," Wella digresses sentimentally, "brown and beautiful with white-blond hair. He liked those wood pegs that come with a hammer.

Wella kept active with the children from the time they were born. Shown here with Aaron in the stroller.
PHOTO COURTESY OF WELLA HARTIG

He'd throw them into the pool if he was mad at me, and they would swell. I don't know how many of those we went through.

"With Hayley, I had to bring *two* playpens," Wella wisecracks, recalling how she hauled two small children and their accoutrements to the pool every day at the Newport Beach Tennis Club in the upscale Eastbluff neighborhood of Corona del Mar. She claims she and Scott could only manage a swim membership at the full-service athletic club, but that gave her a place to work out, and she could feed the kids hot dogs from the little café at the club.

"You have to have those breaks," Wella insists. "I had to do something physical."

In the same way books helped shape her exercise routine, Wella began to

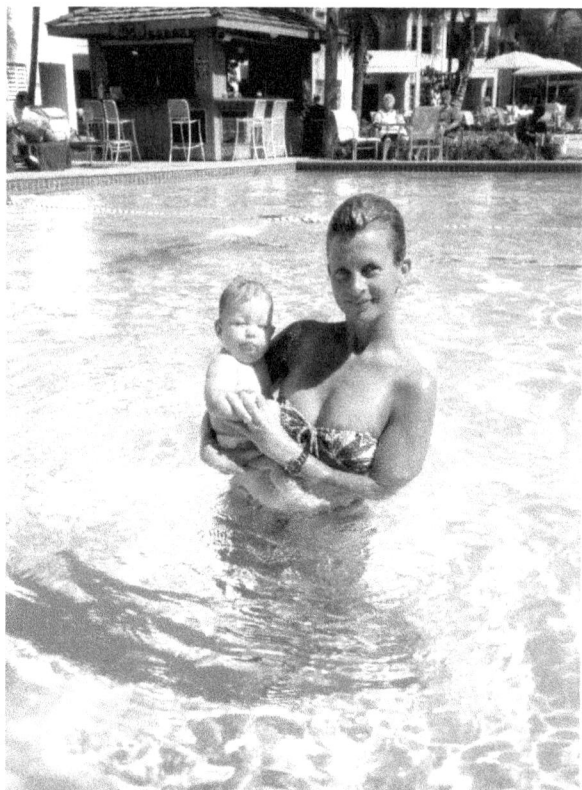

RIGHT: *Wella holds baby Hayley in the water.*
BELOW: *Aaron and a friend play in the pool. On the side are his wooden pegs.*
OPPOSITE: *By six months, Aaron could swim to the lap lines.*
PHOTOS COURTESY OF WELLA HARTIG

read biographies and found she could learn from others whose lives she had admired.

"I learned a lot about life from biographies," she says. "I identified with Kate Hepburn; I could relate to her tomboyish ways. And Jackie Kennedy, I liked how she raised her children. I think I was molded by a lot of what I read." She remembers reading about how people succeeded and absorbing good ideas for parenting, even before she had children of her own.

Neither Aaron nor Hayley had formal swim lessons. However, from the time they were babies, Wella held them in the pool, swishing them around and teaching them to puff their cheeks to hold their breath while putting their faces in the water. Even though the marriage was tense by that time, Scott loved to play with the kids, too, and helped her teach them to swim. He had learned to swim as a baby himself, growing up in Florida with parents who were former swimmers.

"Scott and I would throw Aaron back and forth in the pool when he was only a month old," Wella remembers. "By two months, we'd dip his little face in the water. By six months, he could swim to the lane lines. At a year, he could dive off the board and swim for our car keys. He was like a circus baby! Of course, we were so young and stupid, we didn't know that was bad for his ears—he had a ton of ear infections."

When Aaron learned to swim at six months, Wella wrote in his baby book, "I just know he's going to be the next Mark Spitz."[14] He was a quiet child, Wella remembers, and didn't talk much until he was three, when he suddenly began spouting complete sentences. Perhaps foreshadowing his proclivity for speed, young Aaron's favorite toy was a miniature riding motorcycle that ran on a battery, with an accompanying "gas station" in the backyard. He was also quite smitten with a full-size blue vintage Porsche that Scott acquired.

Darling, wide-eyed Hayley "came out a spitfire, a ball of energy," Wella recalls, in contrast to mellow Aaron. By three months old, Hayley was pulling up on the rings in the crib, trying to stand.

"She looked like Sweet Pea," Wella says, referring to the baby in the old *Popeye* cartoons. "I thought she should still have those baby outfits, like a little sack, and there she was standing in the crib!"

When Hayley was about four months old, Wella heard a thump and rushed in to find Hayley on the rug. She had climbed out of her crib. Hayley started crawling at four months, too, and was cruising between the furniture by seven months. By eight months, she was walking freely.

"She was teeny as could be," Wella exclaims, "with the will of a champion from birth."

Eventually, Scott found a job back in Naples, Florida, selling boats, so the couple left California. For a while, the young family rented a house across the street from the beach, with a nice backyard and a pool.

"Hayley had French doors in her room. She would be in her crib, all sweaty. In California, I would leave the doors open for fresh air but didn't know that in Florida you had to leave the air-conditioning on," Wella says, her voice rising. "So these little geckos would run in and out of the house, and Hayley could catch *geckos* in her crib!" She pauses for effect, holding up an imaginary gecko in surprise, and laughs. "*What* did I have as a child!?

"I really didn't understand the magnitude of Hayley being able to get out. Of course, we had the pool, and the kids were brown as berries, because we lived right across from the beach," she reiterates, explaining how Aaron and Hayley were used to the sun and water. Then one Sunday afternoon, when Hayley was about eight months old, Wella and Scott were weeding in the yard. They thought the children were in the house.

"Aaron came and was pulling, pulling me, trying to say, 'Come,'" Wella begins, then shudders, thinking about what happened next. She followed Aaron, who led her back to the pool.

"I saw Hayley lying in the pool, facedown! I grabbed her up, and"—Wella pauses dramatically to demonstrate frightened eyes, mouth pursed, cheeks full of air—"she had puffed her cheeks, was holding air in her cheeks," just as

Aaron, less than two years old, dives from the board while Wella, pregnant with Hayley, swims laps in the background. PHOTO COURTESY OF WELLA HARTIG

Wella had taught her. Needless to say, after that scare, Wella made sure the doors were locked, with chairs in front of them.

"Honestly, Hayley was just so, *so* coordinated. I cannot explain it any other way. Here was this cute, fat baby sweating up a storm trying to get out of that crib. Driven! Very, very driven," Wella repeats, her voice still tinged with wonder.

Sweet little blue-eyed, blonde Hayley was strong-willed in other ways. At her third birthday, she received some red shorts and a white tank top from a friend at the party. Wella asked Scott to change Hayley into the outfit while the guest was still there to see. As Scott was changing her, Wella recalls that "Hayley said, clear as a bell, 'Stop it, you ass-*hole*.' I couldn't believe it! She picked that time to say *that*! She thought she was being humiliated by having her outfit changed in front of everyone."

Thinking about it a minute, Wella adds, "She still has a very salty mouth. I say curse words when it fits in. Hayley does the same exact thing. It's just her vocabulary. What she says is often comical, profound, but so true. I just love that about her. She just is *Hayley*. She has her own dictionary of words."

One other anecdote from Florida was notably prescient. When Aaron was about four years old, the family visited the Swimming Hall of Fame in Fort Lauderdale. Several years later, when he was about seven, Aaron asked after swim team practice one day, "What would it take to get into the Hall of Fame?" Wella responded offhandedly that it would probably mean breaking a lot of records for a long time. Aaron looked thoughtful. Not long after that, he got a book of swim records, which he pored over. Though he never talked about it, Wella noticed that when Aaron did begin to break records, he would highlight the ones he was trying to break in his book.[15]

"I remember being pretty inspired by what I was seeing, by the history of the sport," recalls the adult Aaron, thinking back to that long-ago excursion to the Swimming Hall of Fame. "I became a bit of a student of the sport, the history and the past of it. And a lot of it, too, wasn't just *swimming* for me. I was growing up around the ocean, and a lot of the guys who first started the sport of swimming were just guys who happened to be good in the water. They happened to be good swimmers, so they went and swam in the Olympics. That's the way it was. When you look back into the 1910s, the 1920s, it wasn't like they were professional swimmers. That's what I respected probably more than anything."

* * *

Three-year-old Hayley, modeling the outfit she protested at her birthday party.
PHOTO COURTESY OF WELLA HARTIG

ASKED WHETHER SHE SEES HERSELF IN HER CHILDREN, Wella hesitates. She remembers that she didn't walk until she was fourteen months, but her family said it was because she was carried everywhere. She was also a giant baby, she says, which might have slowed her down. But she smiles when she recalls that she was a bundle of determined energy, too. Her resolution to raise children differently than her parents did could be part of the same streak of willpower visible in Hayley. Aaron is also incredibly focused, showing perhaps the quieter side of that resolve. Despite her regrets about how her relationship with Scott disintegrated, Wella insists she would not have done anything differently: "Scott was outdoorsy and athletic. Without him, I might not have had the same children that I have."

It was painful for Wella to finally recognize, but the problems between

Aaron and Hayley (about four and two years old, respectively, in this photo) eat snacks in their strollers at Disney World.
PHOTO COURTESY OF WELLA HARTIG

her and Scott were never going to be resolved. She suspected Scott was cheating on her, too. She would clear the car of baby seats and crumbs, so he could drive it to see clients, yet before long, evidence suggested he was holding more clandestine meetings. Though Wella kept hoping things would change, she saw that Scott wasn't ready to take responsibility for having a family, despite having two children to consider. She hesitates even now to say anything about him that would disparage him in their eyes.

The adult Hayley, though, has some thoughts on the subject. Knowing how much more relaxed about life she and her brother are, she suspects they're a little like Scott. "We're so 'go with the flow,' but Mom worries," Hayley reflects. "Well, how could they not clash? They got married when they were young, before they even knew that about themselves. And maybe they couldn't yet deal with it in a mature way. I know how Mom and I clash. And Scott was the type of person who didn't want to settle down. It probably scared him, too."

When Wella's sister Patte, on her way to take her children to Disney World, visited the family in Florida, she spoke very directly, telling Wella to get out of the situation and find a way to support her kids. Aaron was in "transition class," an option between kindergarten and first grade for children with late birthdays, and Hayley was about to start kindergarten. If they left that summer, the kids could start fresh at a new school at the beginning of the school year.

Wella was frightened. She didn't know if she could take care of the kids alone, and she knew Scott could not pay child support. They had moved to Fort Lauderdale, then back to California, and had now returned to Florida. There was always upheaval with each new boat-related job—a sales position elsewhere, or a fancy yacht to live on and fix. "That was all dreamy, if you didn't have children to support," Wella points out, "but you can't raise a family that way."

Although it terrified her to imagine being their sole parent, Wella completely adored her children, and that strong bond finally centered her enough to make a tough decision.

"My kids were very young," she says. "I left early, but not early enough. I knew he'd never be able to help. And I couldn't do it with him. We were no good for each other."

.

Chapter 4 : Guidance

Wella's Tip for Staying Afloat: *Never, ever, ever make kids think they're better than anyone else.*

"WE DIDN'T HAVE A TON WHEN WE GOT TO CALIFORNIA from Florida," Wella begins quietly. "I had separated from their father. And I left—really, it was the only way. It was just a clean break. We basically left with clothes. Aaron had a box of Legos, and Hayley had some dolls. We got on the plane, and we went to California and stayed with my parents."

She recognized that for the children to have a stable home life, she had to leave. "At the time, Scott didn't even know I wasn't coming back," she says. "I didn't know for sure myself."

Aaron was six years old and Hayley four when Wella shepherded them onto a plane bound for California in the summer of 1990. She doesn't know how much they remember, a topic that seems to have been collecting dust under the family furniture for many years. Wella had hoped that they were young enough not to remember too much about that painful period of their lives.

At the airport during the layover, the enormity of the situation hit her. "I remember feeling nervous because I knew in my heart it was over, and he didn't. We had taken very little with us. I think I was oblivious to what could lie ahead. I was just doing baby steps to the airport, baby steps to the grand-parents' house…," she says.

They had arrived very early for the connecting flight, so Wella read to Aaron and Hayley as they fiddled around in the empty waiting area. No one else was there yet. Through the plate glass, Wella could see the plane being readied for their flight.

"I had a strange sense of peace, like maybe this insane life with Scott was finally over," she recounts. "I tried to make the kids excited about Hayley starting school and Aaron beginning at a new one. I held it together during a time when I had no idea how things would turn out." Looking back, she speaks compassionately of her younger self, the brave girl who followed through on leaving, and admits, "*That*, I find pretty strong."

Arriving in California, Wella showed up at her parents' home. If she had expected open arms and coddling from her family, she would have been sorely disappointed. As she remembers it, the morning after she landed, her father drove her downtown in his Cadillac—to the welfare office.

Reflecting on that time, Wella realizes she was just going through the motions and didn't fully understand the significance of what was happening. Her brother had given away or taken as his own all the furniture and art she and Scott had stored when they moved to Florida. He also insisted that she pay rent and utilities for staying in their parents' home.

To go to work and shuttle the kids around, her father let her drive an older-model Volvo, since he owned two other cars. So that no one she knew would see her using food stamps, Wella drove to a different part of town to buy groceries at Stater Brothers—a store with the brightly lettered motto "Lowering Prices Everyday / To help you SAVE on what you pay."

It was humiliating to be on welfare, especially in Wella's experience of sparkly Southern California, where appearances suggested wealth and status. The places where she'd grown up were seemingly bastions of success—beautiful Mediterranean-style homes, gardens of blazing fuchsia bougainvillea, and dazzling ocean views. To be suddenly poor was unspeakably degrading.

"I never had asked Aaron what he remembers," Wella explains now, "but I said the other day, 'Aaron, we came here basically with nothing, almost like immigrants.' And he said, 'I remember. I remember living at Grandma and Grandpa's.'

"I asked him, 'Aaron, did you feel like you didn't have very much?' But he told me, 'No, you took such good care of us in the way that you always kept us busy. We didn't need things, as far as monetary things. You taught us to be outside, rollerblading with you, and then you took us to swimming and we stayed busy that way. You kept our minds and our bodies busy.' He said that helped influence him."

Wella's sister-in-law was trained as a dental hygienist, a career that paid relatively well and could offer flexible hours. Wella returned to Orange Coast College and earned "coronal polish" and "X-ray technician" certificates so she could clean teeth and take dental X-rays. There, she also had a helpful advisor who taught her how to present herself and what would be expected in job interviews. Wella landed the first job she applied for at a dentist's office, where she would work for Dr. Millspaugh for the next seven years. Still, money was tight. Wella continued accepting welfare, working part time to be able to pick Aaron and Hayley up after school and take them to swim practice. Asked why she didn't leave notoriously expensive Southern California for somewhere more affordable, however, she doesn't hesitate: "I was comfortable there. I had always been there."

In California, Irvine is renowned for being utterly planned. Everything looks perpetually new and freshly landscaped, mulched with long pine needles or bark that smells like fresh redwood. Square stucco storefronts are clean and spare, with large plate-glass windows. Instead of tall signs competing with the trees, birds-of-paradise—their orange and blue blossoms resembling the heads of cranes—cluster around the weighty, mahogany signs that sit like cornerstones, announcing each "village" lined with Trader Joe's, Starbucks, Ralph's grocery stores, and nail salons. Development nestles behind carefully shaped hedges and vigilantly tended landscaping. Even the walls buffering the six-lane freeways are draped with bright bougainvillea. It all smacks of clean and modern, if you avert your eyes from the inevitable detritus undulating like confetti ribbons along the sides of the freeway in the eddies from the traffic.

The lines of trees, carefully plotted neighborhoods, well-marked bike paths, and wide streets seem designed for simplicity. While Wella claims to dislike this "island of red in a sea of blue" for its politics and for its uniformity ("Every house looks the same!"), that very structure and orderliness may have held some appeal for her, as it offered the feeling of a family-friendly, safe environment when her own life seemed to be crashing out of bounds.

At times when she didn't have access to the old Volvo, she was determined not to let Aaron and Hayley down—or let them know how desperate circumstances had become. When she had to take the bus, it was incredibly difficult, she recalls, "but I tried to make it into an adventure." Riding the bus, in car-conscious Southern California, felt decidedly "lower class." It was a humbling foray into a lifestyle she never expected to be navigating. In one colleague at her office, though, Wella found an empathetic friend and inspiration.

"Denise had it really hard," Wella recalls. "She knew I was taking the bus. If someone couldn't pick me up, she'd take me home. For her, working forty hours a week and raising two kids on her own, she had to learn to deal. People who've always had curveballs maybe know how to deal with them. She was extremely sweet."

Wella, through reading and serious rethinking of her life, began developing some principles that she hoped would help her teach sound morals to her kids: "Aaron says he remembers when we got in the car, when we'd all be together, when we had our private time away from Grandma and Grandpa, I would try to share my philosophies."

Wella told her children, "The way I look at things, you guys, we're no different than the guy who sweeps the streets, the guy that mows your lawn. Treat them exactly the way you would if you met the president of the United States." Because they attended schools in wealthy communities, Wella knew she needed to start early with this talk. She stressed to Aaron and Hayley, "We're all the same, and you have to always, always remember that. Never think that somebody's better than you or that you're better than somebody. I don't want you growing up with any chip on your shoulder *or* feeling like you're entitled to something."

Wella wanted Aaron and Hayley to develop empathy and humility. She knew she couldn't afford to give them the material goods they saw around them, but she was determined to give them a strong sense of self and a sense that they were equal to their peers.

Despite her circumstances, Wella had big dreams for her kids. She insists, "No matter how bad it was, money-wise—even if I had been living in a shelter—nothing was going to stop me." She was set on raising Aaron and Hayley the way she believed was right.

"I loved my children more than I loved *anything*," she emphasizes. "I never loved anything, didn't know you could love like that. My parents were able to let me go . . ." Wella was determined to be a different kind of mother. She didn't want to pressure her children but fully intended to guide them, as she felt a parent should.

As Wella admired swimmers and enjoyed swimming herself, it seemed natural to her to sign the kids up at the YMCA as soon as she returned to California. The Newport Beach Y has two modest pools behind it, overlooking what locals call "the back bay," a marshy inlet of Newport Beach surrounded by dunes and brushy desert plants.[16] The coach there, Stacey Hand, was a swimmer just out of Pepperdine University in Malibu, who turned out to be a great coach and a friend to Aaron, Hayley, and Wella. Coach Stacey, whose married name is Zapolski, was only twenty-two years old when the Peirsols arrived. Aaron had just turned seven; Hayley was five. Though Coach Stacey had been a backstroker herself at Pepperdine, she didn't start future Olympic backstroke champion Aaron out that way.

Zapolski spent a lot of time with Hayley and Aaron during the year and a half that she coached them. Wella was a single mom then, and Zapolski enjoyed helping her out. Of Hayley, Zapolski writes,[17] "Hayley was a rambunctious little girl with a personality to match. She would say just about anything to anyone and had this cute little pixie blonde haircut. She was the smallest kid on the team but was never afraid to hold her own against the bigger kids, both in and out of the water. She would have me laughing and smiling every day. Many days before practice, she would march herself into my office at the YMCA like she owned the place and would always have a story to tell. She was and still is the epitome of self-confidence."

Aaron had a distinctly different personality, according to the coach: "Aaron was slightly quieter than Hayley, even though he was older. He loved all sports, not just swimming. He was always busy, always on the go. If he got to practice early, he would be out shooting baskets at the outdoor hoops. Aaron had drive and determination like no one I have ever seen at that age. He would push himself every day in practice to keep up with the older and stronger kids. He *loved* working hard!"

Zapolski's comment about Aaron's work ethic has been echoed, independently, by all of the coaches who mentored Aaron over the years. That kind of work ethic plays right into theories about children who are destined to become ultra-achievers. In his book *The Genius in All of Us,* which analyzes the science and psychology of highly successful athletes and achievers, author David Shenk points out that "the single greatest lesson from past ultra-achievers is not how easily things came to them, but how irrepressible and resilient they were.... Uncommon achievement requires an uncommon level of personal motivation and a massive amount of faith."[18]

Contrary to what many of us imagine about the parents behind children who show talent early on, though, Zapolski points out that Wella wasn't pushing her kids. "When the kids first started swimming, Wella didn't want them to compete in swim meets because she was afraid they would burn out," Zapolski recalls. "I laugh often when I think back on that. I literally had to convince her that the meets were like the icing on the cake for them after many days of practice."

Zapolski stresses that kids usually love the swim meets, as long as the parents don't ruin things by putting too much pressure on their young children.

"If more parents would be like Wella, there would not be so many kids burnt out from swimming at young ages," Zapolski comments. "She was able

RIGHT: *Coach Stacy was only twenty-two when Aaron and Hayley started swimming at the YMCA. Here, they pose with medals from a swim meet.* PHOTO COURTESY OF WELLA HARTIG

BELOW: *Aaron and Hayley Peirsol began their swim career at the pool behind the YMCA. The back bay, where Wella ran, shows in the background.* PHOTO: GRETCHEN ROBBINS

to let the kids have fun with the meets."

Despite imposing her affinity for swimming on her two children, Wella learned to step back to see how Aaron and Hayley took to it for themselves. She loved them regardless of their successes, and they understood that. As if validating the approach Wella took, author Shenk writes that "early exposure to resources is wonderful, as is setting high expectations and demonstrating persistence and resilience when it comes to life challenges. But a parent must not use affection as a reward for success or a punishment for failure. The parent must show faith in the child's ability to seek achievement for his or her own inner satisfaction."

Aaron, in his late twenties, underscores the point, saying, "The entire time I swam, I swam because I wanted to. Swimming was for me. I can dedicate it to my family wholeheartedly, but at the end of the day, I didn't swim for anyone else but myself."

Aaron was a natural in the water and, within a short time, was walking away with lots of first-place medals. Zapolski saw the looks he got from jealous teammates. "In order to keep peace on the team, I had to quickly explain to him the importance of humility," she notes. "Once again, Wella was able to instill the sense of pride in her children yet helped them to remain humble as well."

"You have to teach them young to be good losers as well as good winners," Wella says. "Acting too jubilant or crazy as a winner says something, too. Be gracious! Really, those ribbons are just *things*. It's the humility people will remember. Coach Stacey helped, too. We taught him from the beginning."

It was obviously a lesson Aaron took to heart, as he earned over his lengthy career a reputation for being incredibly gracious. Now, still the man to beat in backstroke, hailed as a living legend, "Aaron is the most humble athlete you could ever meet," Zapolski emphasizes. "While he undoubtedly achieved athletic success that the rest of us could only dream of, he does not define himself as a swimmer. Swimming is what he does, but it is not who he is. I think that simple fact is what has helped him to compete for so many years."

Wella could see from the beginning that Aaron seemed born to swim. He never talked about practice, and fairly early on he made the comment that Wella credits as key to the kids' swimming success: Referring to all the parents in the stands, who parsed their children's every stroke at workout, Aaron asked Wella not to interfere. He wanted to tend to business himself.

Wella ran the path around the back bay, officially the "Upper Newport Bay," during the kids' swim practices at the Y. PHOTO: LAURA COTTAM SAJBEL.

Wella took his request for space seriously. "Out on the pool deck, that's their world. We've had our chance, and we need to get out of the way," she observes, with a smile at the irony of the child guiding the parent.

"He may have been doing that all along," she concedes. "He told me to back off. He didn't want me in the fray. He wanted me to drop him off at practice, go do my own things, and come back. Where he got that wisdom, I don't know. I'm really, really blessed. Lucky. That was probably the best advice I've *ever* been given." Aaron wanted her to get on with her life and let him do things on his own. Wella listened, and she used the kids' swim-practice time to run.

"I do remember that circumstance being a very important part of developing the separation between family and swimming," the grown Aaron confirms with a smile.

Hayley, of course, went about practice in her own way. The usual arrangement became that Wella would drop the kids off for practice and take a run around the back bay. When she returned early one time, she couldn't find Hayley in the pool. The coach told her Hayley hadn't come that day. Starting to panic, Wella rushed into the dressing room, where she came across Hayley, meticulously carving her name into a wooden shelf.

"'I didn't feel good. I didn't feel good at all,'" says Wella, mimicking Hayley's explanation in a childlike voice, eyes widened to imitate the five-year-old girl. With a bit of discussion, it came to light that sometimes Hayley would stand in the lockers during the entire practice, then shower before coming to Wella's car, so as not to arouse her mother's suspicion. But those dalliances only lasted a little while.

"That was twenty years ago," Wella says now, brushing off these early incidents of slacking and recounting how hard Hayley later worked under her triathlon coach, Siri Lindley, and all the time she put in for her distance events at Auburn.

Coach Stacey also credits Wella's personal exercise regimen for inspiring her children: "Wella has run and swum every day since I have known her. Her commitment to healthy living and exercise is unbelievable. She has been a positive example to her children every day, since they even watched her swimming laps while in a playpen at the pool!"

Luckily, all around the back bay behind the Y loops a pleasant paved trail, so when Wella left the kids for practice, there was a path to run just beyond the fence.

* * *

BECAUSE OF THE WAY WELLA ARRANGED THEIR SCHEDULE, the kids thought swimming was How Things Were. They started so young, it was just part of life. "Aaron and Hayley have had no other life than training," Wella acknowledges. Her kids swam six days a week, including Saturdays, year round. And Aaron was focused. He could beat the fourteen-year-olds when he was far younger. "He was just born to swim," Wella reiterates.

As they grew, the two of them worked diligently in the pool while other kids were out surfing. "That was hard for Aaron," she comments, thinking back wistfully. "He had to say no to everything." But over time, the kids absorbed the value of hard work, as it began to pay off. They recognized that they could get faster.

To compound things, the area in which they lived was flamboyantly affluent. "Those other kids had Mercedes," Wella clarifies, while she drove Aaron and Hayley around in her parents' aging Volvo. In a move that probably didn't endear her to her parents and siblings, she tried to keep distance between Aaron and Hayley and their cousins, whom she believed were given too much. "I didn't want them [Aaron and Hayley] to see entitlement," she explains, listing fancy cars, Rolexes, and Gucci loafers among the extravagances she could not have afforded for her kids but which she saw heaped on

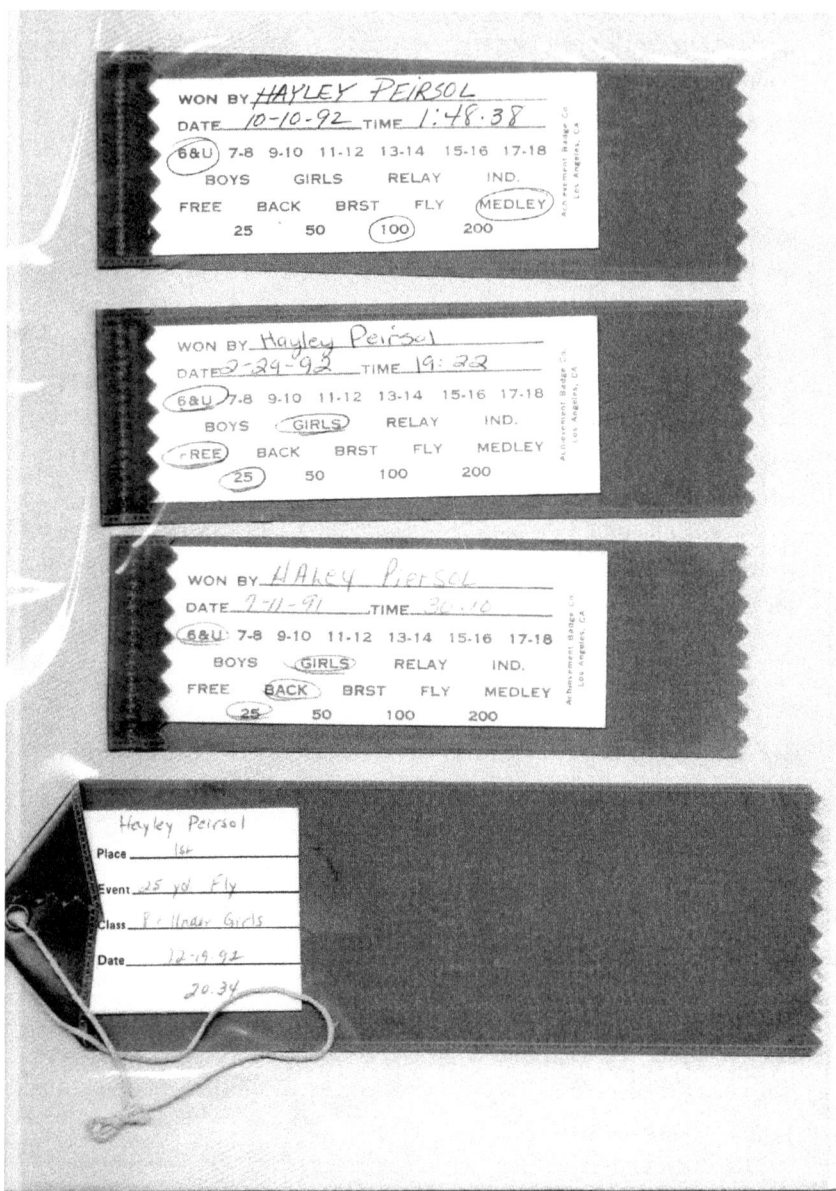

WON BY *HAYLEY PEIRSOL*
DATE *10-10-92* TIME *1:48.38*
(6&U) 7-8 9-10 11-12 13-14 15-16 17-18
BOYS GIRLS RELAY IND.
FREE BACK BRST FLY (MEDLEY)
25 50 (100) 200

WON BY *Hayley Peirsol*
DATE *2-24-93* TIME *19:22*
(6&U) 7-8 9-10 11-12 13-14 15-16 17-18
BOYS (GIRLS) RELAY IND.
(FREE) BACK BRST FLY MEDLEY
(25) 50 100 200

WON BY *HALEY Peirsol*
DATE *2-11-91* TIME *36.16*
(6&U) 7-8 9-10 11-12 13-14 15-16 17-18
BOYS (GIRLS) RELAY IND.
FREE (BACK) BRST FLY MEDLEY
(25) 50 100 200

Hayley Peirsol
Place *1st*
Event *25 yd Fly*
Class *6 Under Girls*
Date *12-19-92*
20.34

These first-place blue ribbons, for the six-and-under age-group races, attest that Hayley showed promise early on—even in tough events such as the Butterfly (FLY), a difficult stroke to master, and the Individual Medley, in which swimmers compete using all four racing strokes.
COURTESY OF HAYLEY PEIRSOL

their friends and cousins.

"I look back, and I don't know how I did it," Wella states, relating the frantic race from work to school pick-up to swim practice. "I worked my tail off and drove the kids everywhere. At the time, it didn't seem like I was sacrificing. It felt like I was doing for them. You just put your head down and never, ever complain or the kids are done. They pick up on that and feel they are a burden.

"Since *my* dreams didn't come true . . ." She pauses, pensive. "I'd get lost in my thoughts when I swam, and I'd pray to God that [my children] would be swimmers and could make it through college on their own."

Chapter 5: Character

Wella's Tip for Staying Afloat: *Jackie Kennedy was right when she said, "If you bungle raising your children, I don't think whatever else you do well matters very much."*

AT SWIM MEETS, PARENTS WERE EXPECTED TO TIME OR KEEP SCORES or write names on the ribbons, and Wella was helping to organize volunteers for the Y. Tim Hartig, whose son, Greg, and daughter, Erin, swam on the team, balked at Wella's request for assistance. He told Wella he couldn't help because it was the only time he could film his kids. She was incensed: Of course, that's what every parent would prefer to be doing, she thought, scathingly. However, soon after that initial meeting, Tim began showing up to swim laps at her regular lap time. He started "chit-chatting," as she puts it, sitting nearby and walking her to the car. On weekends, he suddenly started popping up at practice.

"Usually, I'd buy my kids a snack after practice and that was our Saturday—rollerblading, running, the pool, then we'd head home [to my parents' house] reluctantly," Wella explains. But then, her family and Tim's began to do things together. All four kids would squish into the old Volvo or into Tim's BMW, neither of which was meant to hold that many people in the back.

Tim, too, shares memories of doubling all four children—his and Wella's—into the seat belts and singing along to the radio together. Since the kids already knew each other, things were easier than they might have been. All of the kids corroborate those heady times as among their favorite family memories. Hayley, with her inimitable enthusiasm, gushes, "Greg and I would sit in the back, in the seats that face the rear window. I loved sitting back there so I could see the people behind us. Going to the beach was big—I loved wearing Aaron's Speedos instead of my own bikinis. I wanted so badly to be just one of the boys!"

"When I first met Tim I thought he was very into his kids and kind of distant to me," Wella confides. "I started to see him on the weekends come to play with his kids in the pool. I was surprised to see him there. He was so kind and sweet with his children and really protective, because of his divorce. I thought this was very endearing because you could see how much he loved them."

Tim kept shyly asking her to lunch, and the persistence paid off. "Finally I said yes, and we had *the best* time," she confesses, remembering their first official date in the fall of 1991.

"After that, he would ask to see me with Aaron and Hayley, with his kids, and we would have a wonderful time. So from there it was easy to fall in love, because I felt he loved us all! What more could I want? And he was honest, which I had never had."

"Besides being the cute woman in the white Volvo," Tim says, "Wella was intriguing because she had a certain spunk that I always have admired in women. She could handle my acidic tongue as well as give it right back to me. Her children were her world, and I felt the same way about mine—and so as we got to know each other through our children we were able to forge a relationship. The fact that they enjoyed each other's company made it a lot smoother.

"Aaron and Hayley are her world," Tim asserts. "I was willing to make them my world."

Tall and athletic, a runner and former high school basketball player, Tim has clear blue eyes and an open, friendly manner. A counterbalance to high-strung Wella, he seems down to earth—practical, sensible, and stable. Born in Iowa and transplanted to California, he grew up in an environment completely different from Wella's. According to Tim, his family didn't demonstrate the same drive for "getting ahead" that hers did. His father believed that as long as there was a roof over your family and they were fed, you could be satisfied. Tim characterizes his parents as loving, and Wella and her children definitely benefited from the open-heartedness of Tim's mother, Fran.

Tim—whose disposition is generally upbeat—verifies the unusual nature of Wella's family: "I'd never met people quite like that. Her mother is one of these people who loves in such a weird way. She's so darn negative about everything. Nothing's good enough."

Tim says Wella's father, Joseph, who passed away in May 2009, "liked to drink, but he was a *great* guy. After a couple of drinks, he would recite poetry, orate—some great stories—though when he'd start to talk, you could tell his kids had heard them a million times."

Wella was uncomfortable living in her parents' home with children of
her own. Her mother was still a stickler for keeping the house immaculate,
which meant Wella constantly had to clean up after normal spills and chide
the kids to pick up. Also, being a bit older, her parents preferred calm and
quiet, which made herding two extraordinarily active kids a challenge.

"Aaron and Hayley couldn't just let go and be children there," Wella says.
"And I didn't want my kids to hear all the negative." So she kept Aaron and
Hayley busy and out of their grandparents' house.

For two years after returning to California, Wella had tried to avoid the
issue of Scott Peirsol. She denied visits, refusing to let Aaron and Hayley
fly to see him on their own. She was frustrated and angry, feeling that Scott
rarely sent money to help her support their children and remained preoccu-
pied with his own life. Her parents pressured her, too, to keep the children
away from Scott's influence. However, knowing how Aaron missed his dad,
she finally had a change of heart and let Aaron and Hayley fly to Florida to
see Scott for two weeks in the summer of 1992. When her parents, who were
away on a cruise, heard that she had let the children go, they were furious.
They told her that if Aaron and Hayley weren't back when they returned, she
would lose the Volvo.

She and Tim talked it over, and that week, she moved her stuff and the
kids' into Tim's home.

Tim's father had recently passed away, and his mother, Fran, was living
with Tim and his children. Erin and Greg, in counseling after their parents'
divorce, had chosen to stay the school years with Tim and the summers with
their mom, who had packed up and moved six hundred miles away. Tim
says his mother fully supported the decision for Wella to move in, and that
she provided a doting grandmother figure, for Hayley in particular. Wella,
who has a genuine soft spot for Tim's mom, says that Fran taught Hayley to
read; later, when Fran got fatally sick with brain cancer, Hayley would sit
and read to *her*.

Aaron and Hayley got along really well with Tim's kids, as Wella saw
things. As the kids were already friends from swim team, it was a natural
progression as the two families began to merge. To solve the Aaron/Erin
homonym dilemma, the family referred to them specifically as Aaron Peirsol
or Erin Hartig. They discarded the notion of changing the pronunciation of
either name, as some people suggested. Erin was older and, by all accounts,
very bright and successful at school. Greg was Aaron's age, though smaller in

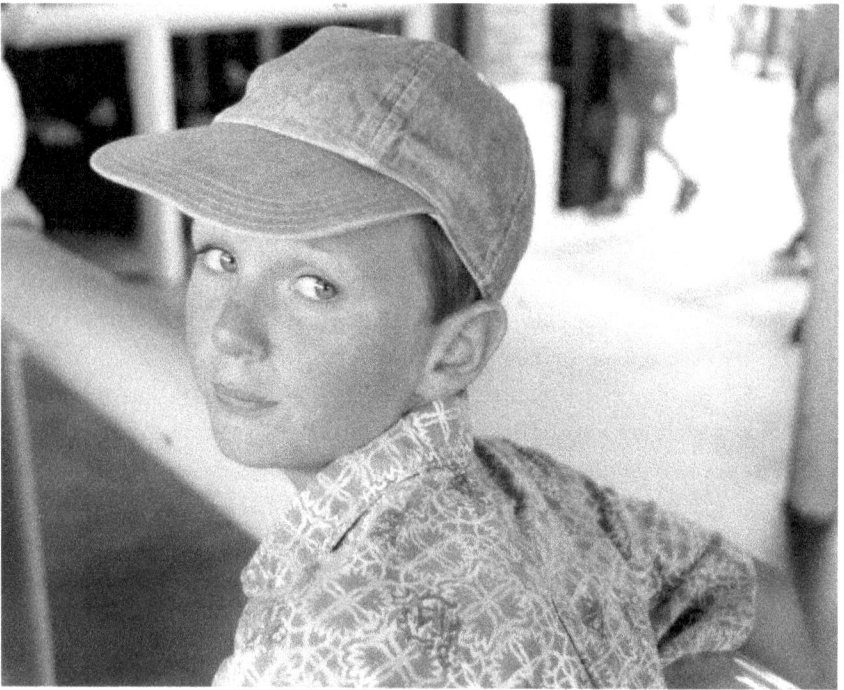

Aaron was about eight or nine when he returned to Florida for a visit with his dad. PHOTO COURTESY OF WELLA HARTIG

stature, and much more leisurely than either of the energetic Peirsol kids.

"Aaron liked to wrestle. He was like a big puppy, and Greg would yell, 'Get him off of me!'" Wella recalls, laughing. "Then, Tim would tell Greg, 'Get back in there and play. That's what boys do!'"

Tim admits that the blending of their families into what he calls the "Brady Bunch" was probably tougher on Erin and Greg than it was on Aaron and Hayley. Erin's and Greg's mother was still involved in their lives; adding a stepmother was complicated.

"Wella was much more structured and maybe even intimidated my Erin," he says. Erin, twelve at the time, had been at her mother's house for the summer when Tim and Wella called to tell her they were moving in together. In retrospect, Tim says, that must have been difficult, because she would be coming home to share her bedroom with a six-year-old sister. "Still, Erin stayed with us through high school, when she went on to Duke. I felt guilt— would she have been better off with her mother? She might say, now, that it was best that she remained with me," Tim says.

"My relationship with my dad is a special one, I think," Erin writes in hindsight. "When I think about my dad, I think about all that he has done for me and all of the sacrifices that he made for his kids. From the time I was ten years old, I lived with my dad and only saw my mom during summers and holidays. My dad was both a mother and father to me for many years. He taught me how to be a great parent and a good person. I know that I always try to make him proud in everything I do.

"My relationship with Wella has had its ups and downs," she concedes. "I think any stepchild's relationship is complicated with their stepparent." While she respects Wella and knows Wella tried very hard to be a good stepmother, Erin concludes, "I actually think that Wella and I are alike in a lot of ways, and sometimes that makes for difficulty in communicating with one another."

While Tim's kids still had a biological mother in the picture, Aaron's and Hayley's father was never around. Tim says it was easy for him to accept Aaron and Hayley as his own and easy for them to accept love from him. And people perceived all the kids as Wella's and Tim's. "They all had mops of white hair, were all beach bummy–looking kids," Tim recalls, smiling. "It was a nice beginning."

"For me, it was so much fun, because my kids are not as aggressive," Tim says. "I used to take Aaron and Hayley into the surf and throw them around or throw sand. Erin and Greg would watch from the sidelines." He remembered that kind of rough-and-tumble play fondly, from when his dad used to toss him around, and was happy to play that way again.

"I became the stability that Aaron and Hayley needed at that time," Tim summarizes. "I've never ever had to question how they feel about me. It's just never an issue."

Aaron agrees. "We moved in with Tim, and the dynamic was changed," he explains. "All of a sudden I had a brother and an older sister and a man who would care for us as his own. We were one big, happy family, as I remember. My fondest memories were of us at the beach when we were younger. My sister would wear my Speedo to the beach and consider herself a boy. Greg and I would watch horror movies in our room. Tim would frighten us here and there by turning the lights off in the house and playing practical, scary jokes. We had dessert almost every night, which I always did love, but we did eat healthy. We eventually got a minivan, which toted all of us around.

"I remember Tim working an incredible amount to support the family at points, something I am, to this day, humbled by... If things changed when we lived with Tim, Erin, and Greg, it was undoubtedly for the better,"

TOP *Hayley (aka Michael) with Greg, buried in sand, and Aaron on Corona del Mar Beach.* PHOTO COURTESY OF WELLA HARTIG

BOTTOM *To release the kids' energy, Wella and Tim set them up to race each other down the beach to what they simply called "the big rock," at the southern end of Corona del Mar Beach.* PHOTO: LAURA COTTAM SAJBEL

Aaron recalls.

"Tim is such an amazing man," vouches the grown-up Hayley. "I could write an entire book on Tim and there would not be one bad thing about him in it. He is our rock, our center in the middle of this teeter-totter."

Erin, too, recalls happy times from that period of her life: "When I look back at the time that I lived with Aaron and Hayley, I have such fond memories of us growing up basically as brothers and sisters. I think we loved and accepted each other pretty easily in that way. We did a lot together and it seems like we always had fun doing anything. I'm sure that... we would fight like siblings tend to do, but I don't have any negative feelings about any aspect of my relationship with either Aaron or Hayley during that time."

As Aaron mentioned, one thing Wella and her kids had always enjoyed was watching scary movies: "I'd be scared, but it was just great being scared," she exclaims with an impish grin. Erin, too, would watch, but she would be hiding, while Greg stood in the hallway, yelling, "I'm watching!" However, Wella says, "My kids would be right up there perched on the edge of their seats in front. Not that Aaron didn't have nightmares—he 'saw' aliens and would crawl in with the girls. Hayley still loves scary movies." One might wonder if Aaron and particularly Hayley and Wella aren't adrenaline junkies, given their proclivity for living on the edge. Wella would call it a personality type—scared of nothing.

Tim sees it from another angle. He surmises that Aaron and Hayley showed "curiosity that bordered on fearlessness—no fear of trying anything. They were open to any and all experiences. That's a great trait."

Hayley, the baby of the family, was probably the toughest kid in the house. She always wanted short hair and wanted to be one of the boys, a fact that rings a bell for anyone familiar with Wella's childhood wish for a "boy cut." Tim and Wella can hardly keep from cracking up as they talk about Hayley stealing Aaron's swimsuits to wear to the beach without a top, even until she was nine years old. People would always comment on "all those cute boys, especially Michael," as Hayley insisted on calling herself. She had cut the long hair off her beautiful doll, whom she had also named Michael— another refrain from Wella's girlhood Barbie-haircut games. Wella and Tim tried to get Hayley to at least wear cute, frilly pink bathing suit bottoms, but she would steadfastly filch from Aaron.

"He would say, 'She's wearing my trunks again,'" Wella says in a deep-voiced imitation of Aaron, then giggles. "Little did he know she had his Speedos on underneath his trunks."

"Hayley was such a little tomboy. Bonding was quick and easy with her," says Tim warmly.

Wella chimes in, "She needed a daddy. She would shinny up and sit on Tim's lap." However, when Tim and Wella set the kids up at the beach to race to one particular big rock, Hayley could beat the boys every time.

"I was just so incredibly feisty," Hayley explains, looking back. "There was no way I would let my brothers beat me and I don't think I ever doubted for a second that I could beat them. I thrived in competing with my siblings, mostly my brothers. Just because I was a girl, I didn't want to be treated any differently... to be coddled or babied... I just wanted to be a tough cookie."

Aaron was growing really quickly during those years, with a shoe size that corresponded to his age: Men's size ten at age ten, size eleven at eleven, up to size thirteen at age thirteen. That growth coincided with his speed. "He was going so fast in the pool," Wella emphasizes.

Wella recalls Aaron holding Tim's hand and swinging it—"Remember, he was still a little boy in many ways"—but his head was already at the height of six-foot-tall Tim's shoulder, and it must have struck people as odd. Greg was closer in size to Hayley, though he was Aaron's age.

One time, not long after they moved in together, Wella went to have her hair done while Tim took the kids rollerblading. As Tim recalls, "Aaron jumped one small puddle and fell wrong." Aaron had broken his arm, a compound fracture.

Wella went ballistic. "I couldn't believe Tim had had done that to my children!" she says, still with a hint of hysteria elevating her voice. "I thought Aaron would never be the same. Tim got to see my manic, crazy side because I was letting him have it—'I can't believe you ruined Aaron's life!' You have to remember," she confides, "that I had Aaron at twenty-six. I was still a baby."

Tim adds, to temper the retelling, "In the car on the way to the hospital, Aaron kept saying, 'Mom, it's okay.'"

Aaron was out of the pool for a while with the break. He was about nine years old, and he missed the Junior Olympics.[19] That he had qualified for the prestigious regional swim meet indicates that Aaron was already posting outstanding times, and Wella knew he was disappointed he would not be able to go. The accident happened around the Fourth of July, so Aaron missed the fireworks, too.

* * *

DURING THE SUMMERS, WHILE ERIN AND GREG LEFT TO VISIT THEIR
mother, Wella signed Aaron and Hayley up to participate in Junior Guards,
a California organization that promotes ocean-safety skills. A three-week-
long day camp for ages eight to seventeen, the program teaches first aid,
CPR, rescue techniques, and surfing. Local community members pitch in to
offer interpretive and educational presentations. Junior Guards trains kids
to handle themselves safely in a variety of situations on the ocean, builds
teamwork and self-respect, and promotes increased awareness of the coastal
environment.[20]

Because they lived so near the ocean, Wella felt Junior Guards was
invaluable for the kids and well worth the expense. The program helped
build character and confidence and skills necessary for living close to the
water. Still, there were times when it was a stretch to cover the costs and
make ends meet. She asked both her dad and Scott to help with that expense
at times, but rarely did they contribute. Tim points out that sometimes
Wella's dad would be in a good mood and offer to help, though usually the
follow-through "never quite happened."

Later on, when she had moved the kids to a more competitive swim club,
Wella recalls that the coaches weren't thrilled when Aaron and Hayley participated in Junior Guards during the summer, because they missed some
swim practices. During the summer, competitive teams held two-a-days
(two practices per day), for a total of four hours of practice. But Wella felt so
strongly about the merits of Junior Guards—and Aaron and Hayley enjoyed
it so much—that they bucked the system. Erin even participated one year in
Junior Guards with Aaron and Hayley, when she was older, and held a job as
an assistant lifeguard for a while.

Despite the fact that they didn't have the exceptionally fast times that
Aaron and Hayley were starting to have, Erin and Greg enjoyed swim team.
They each had their own sets of friends, and Erin continued swimming all
the way through high school. "It gave me a good group of friends, good
exercise, and a way to decompress from the stresses of school," says Erin.
Though there was definitely a disconnect at the athletic levels, Tim and
Wella thought the children seemed accepting of that difference, and they
made a point not to talk about swim workouts or to overemphasize wins.

Asked how Wella and Tim handled the various levels of success the
siblings had at the pool, Aaron comments, "They more or less let me handle
[the outcomes] and they were there as support, which I did need as I was
growing up... I could not say how it affected the other kids. Everyone always

JUNIOR GUARDS

A page out of Hayley's scrapbook includes Junior Guard photos. At top, Aaron, a friend, and Hayley wear the easily spotted yellow caps, of which Hayley was not especially fond. In the bottom photo, Hayley stands, hand on hip, with Aaron two to the left of her. COURTESY OF HAYLEY PEIRSOL

Hayley, about age nine, at the beach. On the pink bookmark,
she got the autograph of water polo great Chris Duplanty.
COURTESY OF HAYLEY PEIRSOL

seemed to have their own thing going on in life, and their own interests. I thought Erin was a great swimmer, and she was academically the best in the family. Greg left as it kicked up to the next level. And Hayley was a great swimmer in her own right. No one kid stood out in the family as any more important, and still doesn't."

Erin, understandably, saw it from another perspective: "I'm sure that [handling the differences among the four kids] was very difficult for Wella and Tim," she acknowledges now that she is a parent herself. As a teen at the time, though, "I always felt that I was being compared to Aaron's and Hayley's successes as swimmers and was found lacking. However, I'm sure a lot of that was due to my own insecurities. I have a feeling that Aaron and Hayley might say that they were compared to me in the realm of academics, but I am not sure. I can say that both my dad and Wella expected the best out of all of us in every situation."

* * *

REAL LIFE IS RARELY SIMPLE. IN THE MIDST OF A LOVE STORY with Tim that has now lasted a couple of decades, there were still a few thorns for Wella. Scared that Scott would get custody, she didn't file for divorce for many years, long after she and Tim had begun raising their blended family together. Then again, Scott never filed for divorce or custody either, although he had moved on to another relationship himself. Wella would not file official divorce documents until 1999, once the kids were of age to decide for themselves where to live.

While it's easy to criticize her handling of affairs, she was dealing with personalities she knew well. Many years later, Scott's father made a visit to California, during which Tim maintains Fred shook his hand and thanked him. Not long after, Fred Peirsol mailed a letter, dated August 2003,[21] to an attorney colleague in California, exploring the possibility of suing Wella for keeping the children from Scott. At the time of that letter, Hayley was eighteen and Aaron twenty; Aaron had already medaled in his first Olympics. Fred Peirsol passed away before the suit came to fruition, but perhaps this incident illustrates why Wella handled matters the way she did.

On April 22, 2004—Earth Day, she recalls—Wella, in a white sundress, picked Tim up early from the office, and they drove to the Old Orange County Courthouse in Santa Ana. No longer used for trials, the quaint building, constructed of reddish sandstone and granite and surrounded by a

Wella and Tim, not long after moving in together.
PHOTO COURTESY OF WELL HARTIG

park-like lawn and waving palms, is a State of California Historic Landmark, and is also on the national registry of historic places as Southern California's oldest court building. The site, which "has been witness to many of the events which shaped present day Orange County,"[22] now rules on passports and official records. The building oversaw one more historic event that day in its marbled halls: the official wedding of Tim and Wella Hartig.

"We had talked about it for years," Wella explains. "It was time. We didn't even tell the kids, although we knew the kids wanted that. They needed to know we were married for life. So we celebrate two dates. Tim first asked me out on November 5, 1991, and then we got married April 22, 2004."

Between the two of them, Wella and Tim tried to raise their family in the ways they believed would be best for all the kids. Tim summarizes their choices: "My father was thankful to have a roof over our head, but we wanted our kids to be told that there are reasons why you reach farther and work harder. To reach for goals was something I decided to teach my kids. We wanted them to go away from home for college. Both Wella and I stayed close to home, which didn't give us an environment to grow. But I knew from my own mistakes that I would get them out, to be uncomfortable, to grow.

"And we wanted them to know it was important to be a good person. We were more interested in character than in accomplishments."

Chapter 6 : Humility

Wella's Tip for Staying Afloat: *You have to take responsibility for what you raise. You have to raise a person, not just a swimmer.*

MEANWHILE, AARON BEGAN TO POST *REALLY* FAST TIMES IN THE POOL.
By 1993, Coach Stacey at the Y was leaving to get married, and Wella had been looking around at other swim programs, knowing that Aaron and Hayley in particular needed more now, in the way of coaching. Because she knew Coach Ted Bandaruk from her days at Orange Coast College, she and Tim took all four kids to swim with Bandaruk's summer-league swim program in Newport Beach. Right away, Wella grew anxious to move on, feeling that this still wasn't enough challenge for Aaron and Hayley.

Wella had heard of the Novaquatics swim program in Irvine—often referred to simply as "Nova"—and decided the family should check it out. Nova was a hotbed of talented swimmers. Its coaches had built a reputation for turning out some of the fastest kids in the nation, and the program demanded excellence in everything from workouts to volunteers. Some people drove two hours to have their kids practice with the team. At that particular time, Wella estimates Nova had at least thirty swimmers with outstanding records.

Nova swimmers practiced at the fabulous Heritage Park Aquatic Center, right next door to Irvine High School. The Heritage Park complex encompasses a recreation center, athletic fields, and tennis courts and is landscaped with lush green grass, tall trees, a central pond, and clean, modern lines. The aquatic center, renovated in 2004 and renamed the William Woollett Jr. Aquatics Center, has been billed as one of the premier swimming venues in the country. It includes three pools—a smaller multi-use pool and two Olympic-size pools that measure 25 yards by 50 meters—to accommodate both short- and long-course races. In 1984 the center had hosted the XXIII Olympiad's pentathlon event.[23] Outdoors in the California sun, under the swaying eucalyptus and palm trees, would have been a pleasant place to practice.

"We just had to go, because Aaron was busting at the seams. He was so good in the water. When we got to Nova and saw all those kids and all that structure, Aaron's eyes were moons! The facility was big and beautiful. But Hayley was reluctant, maybe intimidated," Wella remembers.

Hayley could be shy, despite her outsized personality at home and at the Y. Confident and witty among her familiar swim friends, she nonetheless turned into a wallflower on the playground at school, for example. Wella recalls a kindergarten conference in which the teacher alerted her that Hayley and another little girl were standing against the building during recess, watching the other kids play. Wella couldn't take off work to check on things, but once Tim stepped into the picture, he began making a point of taking lunch to Hayley at school one day a week and eating with her, trying to help her feel more comfortable.

On that first visit to Nova, Aaron swam a workout under Brian Pajer, who coached swimmers aged nine to twelve. Hayley, because of the age grouping, was with different kids under the direction of a female coach who was yelling through a bullhorn. That seemed to be a deal-breaker for Hayley, so Wella and Tim decided not to switch everyone just yet. Then Aaron had the rollerblading crash that broke his arm that summer, so he took a break while it healed.

As they cast about for how to properly channel the speed and gumption they saw in the kids, Wella and Tim couldn't yet fathom what they were facing—either in the labyrinth of competitive swimming or in the enormous potential brimming in Aaron and Hayley. One anecdote illustrates how much they still had to learn. When Aaron's arm had healed, Wella and Tim decided to enter the kids at a youth swim meet held at nearby Golden West College, just for fun, independent of any team. The Pumpkin Meet, scheduled in October, actually awarded pumpkins to the winners of each race.

"We didn't understand the world of swimming at all. We had no idea how it worked," begins Wella.

Tim chimes in, "We just walked up and said we'd like to sign the kids up to swim in the meet." The registrars sitting at the table were incredulous that these parents hadn't followed proper channels, and Tim and Wella had to jump through a few hoops to get the kids registered. "No one would guide us!" Wella exclaims, though eventually the judges let the kids swim.

On the pool deck, Tim and Wella spotted Brian Pajer, the coach whom

Aaron outside their kitchen window, holding his
winnings from the Pumpkin Meet at Golden West College.
PHOTO COURTESY OF WELLA HARTIG

they had met at Nova during their visit the past spring. Completely unaware
of their faux pas, they asked Brian if he would warm up Aaron and Hayley
for the races. Kindly, Brian did so, despite the fact that the kids were not part
of his team. Tim and Wella were grateful, but even more so later, when they
realized that Brian had really gone out of his way to help them when he was
the paid coach of the other swimmers.

Pajer[24] confirms that he noticed a name he didn't remember from previous meets, a boy entered with strong times for his age.

"I was interested to see how Aaron would race against our boys. I
remember the hundred-meter individual medley race in particular," Pajer
recalls. "Aaron and our two best nine-and-ten boys swam in three lanes next
to each other, and Aaron did very well, splitting our guys and taking second
place. I believe Aaron got to know our boys on the first day of the meet, and
Tim and Wella asked me if they could warm up with our swimmers on the
second day of the competition."

Needless to say, "Aaron and Hayley came home with a bunch of pumpkins," Tim recalls, smiling.

Generally, it becomes evident over time which kids in a community are
speedy in the pool, but Aaron and Hayley had been participating in smaller
meets and had not yet shown off their talents for the swim community at
large. Tim says that local *Los Angeles Times* reporter and fellow swim parent

Erik Hamilton[25] later told him that other parents were grumbling that Aaron and Hayley, who were whipping the competition, had appeared out of nowhere. He confided that the buzz among other parents was, "Are they aliens?"

However, that meet illustrated for Aaron that there were faster times to be had and some good competitors out there, and it spurred him to think about his goals. And Wella clearly recognized the difference that good coaching and competition could make for the kids.

The family decided it was time to make the move to a competitive organization with a strong reputation, so they registered the kids at Nova the autumn of 1993, when Erin was thirteen, Aaron and Greg were ten, and Hayley was eight. Coach Pajer recalls Tim and Wella as being quite likeable from their first meeting, an impression that never changed over the years. His words help illustrate the family dynamic and its role in the kids' success: "After getting to know the family better, I thought they were a great combination of personalities. Tim and Wella were very fitness-minded themselves and understood the commitment necessary to excel in sports. Wella was always the worrier and needed to be reassured now and then about Aaron's and Hayley's progress, and she was always a little nervous when they competed in big meets."

And he points out what was becoming evident in the parenting team. "Tim was the perfect fit for Wella's personality, as his steady demeanor and endless patience was a very steadying force for her and the kids," Pajer says. "Tim understood Aaron well, and knew when he needed a little extra push (which was not very often), and when to step back and allow Aaron to discover his own path.

"Tim was also very good at knowing how to handle a certain very young and intense coach—me," Pajer continues, with self-deprecating humor. "He knew when to step in and communicate things that would help me understand Hayley and Aaron better, while also keeping enough distance to let both kids take ownership of their swimming. Aaron and Hayley are very lucky to have Tim and Wella as parents, and I truly believe much of their success in swimming was a result of this great family unit.[26]

* * *

SWIMMING, NATIONALLY, IS A HIGHLY STRUCTURED age-group program, though there are a few local variances. The national model sets different time standards for ages—an A time standard is faster than B times or C times, which essentially begin at entry level. As swimmers advance, there are other goals to achieve, such as Junior Olympics or Junior and Senior National time standards. When Aaron and Hayley swam at Nova, "Q" was a state standard for the Q Meet, a qualifying meet to select an all-star team from southern California to compete against northern California. That meet had the toughest age-group time standard, and its qualifiers were the top two percent of swimmers in the state.[27]

The time standards help to control the size of meets and give swimmers motivational tools to advance. According to Coach Dave Salo, who led the Novaquatics staff and currently serves as head coach at the University of Southern California in Los Angeles, there are about 14,000 age-group swimmers in southern California. In that part of the world, so close to the ocean, the sport has been popular and competitive all along. Though the sport of swimming has increased in visibility nationally, most of the expansion Nova has seen is from growing their own program to accommodate more swimmers. When Aaron and Hayley were practicing at Heritage Park, Nova had only one facility, with about 450 kids on the team, swimming staggered practice times. Today, Nova boasts 700 swimmers at four facilities. Workouts are once a day, year-round, for twelve-and-under swimmers, but when kids hit the advanced group, they begin twice-daily workouts two or three times a week.

"By the time Aaron was in my group, he would do two or three additional morning workouts per week, with regular evenings and Saturdays," clarifies Salo.

* * *

AS THE PEIRSOL-HARTIG FAMILY made the transition into Nova, Tim and Wella began to grasp the pecking order within Southern California Swimming, the local committee (under the auspices of USA Swimming) that oversees official swim times and regulations.[28] Swimmers had to post specific event times to qualify for A, B, or C meets. However, Aaron was swimming Q times by the time he was in the 11–12 age group, indicating that his speed qualified him for the all-star team. To make Coach Pajer's group, the kids had to swim three events with double-A times within a year; Pajer only worked with talent of a particular caliber.

The swimmers on the entire team were so strong that "the team would go to championship meets and it would be a wipeout. It was really great because the kids could feed off each other's momentum," Wella says.

Even then, Aaron was special.

"He definitely had a combination of traits that I had not seen before in one swimmer," Coach Pajer remembers. "He had the physical attributes that you look for in a great swimmer. This includes good flexibility, big hands and feet, good coordination, and good muscular power. He also was very coachable. He had a good natural feel for the water, but was also willing to change his technique if we thought it would help him improve."

Pajer echoes, too, a key trait that all of Aaron's coaches mention: "Aaron was a very hard worker. He was able to train at a high effort level day after day, without letting that effort cause him mental or emotional stress."

Pajer concludes, "For one athlete to have all of these attributes is very unusual. For a ten-year-old boy to already possess this combination of traits at such a young age is unique in my experience."

One particular incident Pajer remembers may have changed the course of swimming history. "Swimming backstroke well takes a good natural body posture, good shoulder anatomy to catch the water properly, and a very strong kick," Pajer explains. "Aaron had all three of these attributes." While working on backstroke, the coach had the swimmers get out and asked Aaron to demonstrate a couple of lengths of backstroke for the rest of the group. Something surprising occurred to Pajer.

Pajer had meant to critique the stroke, to give constructive feedback after the swim as a means for all the swimmers to watch and learn. "As I watched, I took his stroke apart and analyzed his body position, posture in the water, kick form and rhythm, recovery position, pull depth, stroke acceleration, head position, and hand catch. For the first time since I began coaching age-group swimmers, I couldn't find anything wrong with a swimmer's stroke."

It wouldn't be the last time Aaron surprised a coach. Pajer felt a bit overwhelmed, though he never let on. "I felt I had nothing as a coach I could contribute to Aaron at that moment that could improve what I had just seen," he says. "That moment made me realize that from then on, I would probably learn more about backstroke from watching Aaron swim than he would learn from me."

Coach Pajer called in Wella and Tim, suggesting for the first time that Aaron might be a backstroker. "He flipped Aaron over," Wella remarks, referring to the change. Within six months, still only ten, Aaron broke the national age-group record in the 100-meter backstroke event during a summer meet at Cypress Junior College.

Wella was at one end of the pool during that meet, where she could see the clock, and Tim was at the other end of the pool, where Aaron finished.

"I was running to see [Aaron]," Wella says, describing the scene immediately after the race. "I wanted to see the look on his face, because it meant *everything* to him to set that time. This was his last chance to get that record before moving up to the 11–12 age group. When he did it—and people didn't set a lot of records back then—it was the beginning. Then the records started coming. He'd set a goal and get it. You just knew he was going to go for it."

Not knowing how this record-breaking business worked, Wella asked a USA Swimming[29] official at the meet, a woman named Mary Jo, whether Aaron's time would be written up in the new record book. According to Wella, Mary Jo told her, "I think so, but I wouldn't be too happy if I were you. In all my years of being an official, it's always bad when they set records early." Wella was so disappointed that she cried and confided in Tim—never telling Aaron—that this early lead could mean Aaron would not be fast later.

As an adult, Aaron agrees with Mary Jo on the statistics. "She was right," he verifies, explaining that she was probably just trying to harness Wella's expectations.

Many years later, in New York, when twenty-two-year-old Aaron was to be awarded USA Swimming's hugely prestigious Swimmer of the Year for 2005[30], Mary Jo happened to share a cab with Wella and Tim and then followed them into the limo that was waiting for Aaron and his family.

"How's *that*?" Wella asks, still incredulous at the irony of the situation.

* * *

A SHIFT AWAY FROM UNSTRUCTURED PHYSICAL PLAY IN AMERICAN society has paralleled a rise in the intensity of children's sports. Kids are shepherded into organized sports or camps from an early age, a far different experience from impromptu pick-up games at the park. The mindset seems to be that as soon as a child is exposed to a sport (or to music or academics), the goal is to be the best.

Unless the child drives this goal, something is lost, though, in that push for perfection. The sacrifices of a family weigh on a child who is aware of the money and effort heaped on his potential success. After sinking resources into a particular sport, parents feel they've upped the ante and often lock in on the child's accomplishment as reward. Furthermore, parents who praise every small success skew the child's developing sense of self, suggesting that achievement is the only goal. That pressure to succeed can make it hard for a kid to enjoy the sport.

"I would recommend *not* to talk about swimming with your kids," Wella advises. "Those kids"—the ones whose parents were the driving force—"ended up quitting or getting out. Parents would get up in the bleachers and bicker about who was getting attention and not getting enough attention. A lot of jealously went into play."

Tim agrees. "When you fixate, you find ways to make things happen," he says, referring to how he and Wella had to scramble to support the kids. "But Wella's right about internalizing those thoughts. Tell your spouse, but not the neighbors. We never let the kids know that's what we were thinking. If Aaron had never *been* an Olympic champion… well, we didn't put that pressure on the kids."

Though Wella claims she didn't interfere with the kids' practices, she also admits that "the kids were my life." To distinguish between *encouraging* and *pushing*, Tim defines Wella's style of managing the kids at the pool: "You get on the train with Wella. The train leaves the station and it's 'Go.' The kids were never told, 'You have to go.' It was an unspoken expectation, but the kids were never made to feel they wouldn't be loved if they didn't.

"Wella has this ability, and you get on board with it. It's just an energy she has, that has people wanting to keep up. Because they enjoyed practice— the process, the people involved—we were very fortunate. The kids were on board from the get-go. The worst we ever had to do was make Hayley go to practice when she was seven or eight."

Wella recognized the need not only in herself, but in her kids, that set the pace for the family's lifestyle.

"We ran and swam while we had all four kids, before work, and then I would walk at lunch," Wella recalls of her own boundless energy that fueled what Tim calls "the train."

"With Hayley, later, we had to get rid of all that energy!" Wella exclaims. "What would we have done without the pool to burn that energy? She would have gotten into trouble."

Wella did dog the coaches over the years, worrying about the progress and well-being of Aaron and Hayley. She wanted to be sure her children were doing well yet not being pushed too hard. Nevertheless, she made a concerted effort to keep her concerns out of earshot of Aaron and Hayley. Though the adult children tease their mother for worrying so much, for young Aaron and Hayley, her efforts apparently succeeded.

Aaron confirms, "I didn't feel any responsibility to anyone to continue to swim. If anything, I thank my parents for giving me something that was my own, and they let it be my own, and in the process I knew how much they gave me in order to do it."

Hayley agrees. "I loved being given the opportunity to push myself beyond limits that I never even knew existed or ones that I viewed as insurmountable," she says. "I thrived on competing… on accomplishing a goal that I had been working toward for so long. I most definitely would get a high, this complete body high, from competing both in practice and in competition. I loved that feeling of surprise when I barreled through a barricade. It was so rewarding in that way, because it develops character."

All the children must have recognized eventually the sacrifices it took to keep them on the team and in the races. Besides typical costs for raising a family, feeding hungry athletes was a challenge and an expense. With practices at different times, eating together was impossible. Wella jokes about her lack of cooking prowess, but what she and Tim managed worked just fine.

"We had really simple meals—burritos, chicken tacos, spaghetti, chicken with rice, and always a salad," Wella remembers. "And soups, like bean or chicken. I got all our food at a health-food market, so that even if we used packaged items due to time constraints, it would be something like a soup mix, and we'd add lentils or carrots."

She and Tim often had to eat first and keep the food heated for Aaron and Hayley, whose practice ended later, and for Erin, whose practice during high school ended latest of all.

"It was a definite sacrifice, that we couldn't all eat together," Wella says, although everyone has fond memories of the chocolate-chip pancakes that were their traditional race-day fare.

Despite all the scheduling difficulties and long hours of practice, Wella wanted home to be nurturing and loving, the place to chill. She and Tim tried to leave the competition at the pool, creating a respite completely away from talk of practice and coaches' expectations.

"When I was done with practice, it was the last thing I wanted to think about until I was at practice again the next day, and when I was home I wanted to be home," Aaron says now. "My mom was incredibly insightful, I feel, to understand that that was what I, as an individual, needed."

"Even at dinner now," the grown Hayley agrees, "Aaron and I wouldn't talk about times or swimming. In the scheme of things, with all that is going on,

Tim, here with a fellow Nova parent, became the chef at swim meets, whipping up his famous chocolate-chip pancakes on the grill.
PHOTO COURTESY OF WELLA HARTIG

it's almost selfish. You need to be more well-rounded than that."[31]

Besides watching movies with the family, Hayley's form of kicking back was curling up on the couch under a blanket with a book. Tim says that he and Aaron spent a lot of time talking.

"Aaron and I were always having philosophical discussions," Tim notes. "I remember recognizing that I'm talking with this twelve-, thirteen-year-old, who has *good* philosophical questions." He points out that curiosity is what separates great athletes or thinkers, people who look for ways to make things work. "Curiosity and thinking good things—that perpetuates itself. Time after time, that works for Aaron. It's just the way he handles all of us, lives his life, wanting to understand things. He's a deep thinker."

Tim may have identified an attitude crucial to Aaron's success. Author David Shenk writes of the critical nature of "deliberate practice," a factor that raises the bar on repetition: "Deliberate practice requires a mind-set of never, ever, being satisfied with your current ability. It requires a constant self-critique, a pathological restlessness, a passion to aim consistently just beyond one's capability… and a never-ending resolve to dust oneself off and try again and again and again."[32]

As Coach Stacey and Coach Pajer had observed, Aaron loved working hard. Aaron, deflecting credit, compliments his coaches and peers. "I was on a team with a great culture of hard work and kids who were already very talented and very good," he points out. "I also had some very good, very tough coaches who expected a lot and who let me know what it might take to be good." From a young age, he was surrounded by success and says he decided, "If I am going to do this, I may as well do it right.'"

Dave Salo, who coached Aaron after he moved up in the age groups, notes, "Aaron just liked coming to practice, being with his teammates and friends. He liked to work hard and accomplish, to practice what he was capable of doing."

"Aaron and Hayley were both nationally ranked from a young age," Tim points out, which definitely affected the family. Erin and Greg had less competitive personalities, but within the swim team, each of the kids had his or her own group of peers. There were so many swimmers on the team, and the kids seemed to understand and accept that Aaron and Hayley were different, so their extraordinary success in the pool never became a point of overt contention at home, at least not that Tim and Wella noticed.

"Swimming doesn't define you. It's not who you are," Wella says. "We never turned it into a parade. There are children who might be disappointed at not having a big celebration, but the flip side is parents making a flap over every success. That sets kids up to feel that their accomplishments are why they are loved and get fanfare."

Coach Brian Pajer confirms he saw the results of this philosophy, recalling how seamlessly Aaron handled both success and disappointment during his young swimming years. "After seeing Aaron break a record or reach a goal he had set for himself, I could see he was very satisfied with himself and happy with his performance. He was never boastful and was always quick to refocus and set new goals for himself," Pajer says. "When he had a swim he wasn't happy with, Aaron was quick to find out what he needed to do to improve for the next swim. He came to practice the next week ready to work harder than ever to keep moving towards his goals."

Wella and Tim tried to guide all four kids to realize that swimming was only one facet of their lives, but Erin recalls, "The part that I enjoyed least about swimming was the knowledge that I wasn't a very good swimmer, especially in comparison to my siblings."

The tools in Wella's parenting toolbox weren't sized for everyone. While

Hayley, Aaron, and Greg in the yard.
PHOTO COURTESY OF WELLA HARTIG

he admits that his dad tried to treat everyone equally, Greg had a different temperament and different ideas than Wella about how to spend his time. Nearing thirty, Greg reflects, "Life revolved around Wella, Aaron, and Hayley. Being as they were good at swimming, that meant our lives revolved around swimming. I was not able to be a child. I was not able to go play with friends after school because we had to go to swimming. With my mom I was able to be a kid and go do things other than swimming.

"I did like swimming while I did it. But after a while it turned into more of a job, and the fun was taken out of it."

Greg's mother, at some point, "put the tug on him to come live with her, saying he wouldn't have to do swim team," says Tim. He and Wella kept the kids active all the time, "but Greg was more prepared to sleep in and watch TV." He intimates that Wella kept everyone moving with chores and activities. When they weren't swimming, the family was racing to the big rock at the beach or rollerblading. Greg, who never was enthusiastic about the pace of this particular household, left after about a year of swimming at Nova.

"So at ten years old, he decided to go live with his mom," Tim says, still visibly sad. Tim grudgingly acquiesced, insisting that Greg keep up his grades and some activity. "He would have been better off staying with us, in many ways," he laments.

As the years passed, the separation between Tim and Greg grew, but during that period, Tim fulfilled the role of father Aaron needed. "I lost a son, and Aaron had lost a dad," he says.

Tim struggles with this turn of events. "I'm still close with Greg," he comments, almost defensive. "That's a connection that can never go away. But it helped that both Aaron Peirsol and I have each other. That [circumstance] was important for that kind of bonding."

Erin continued to swim through high school, as well as keeping straight A's all along. She was accepted at and decided to attend Duke University, listed then among the top five universities. Later, when Aaron hit high school, Erin left for college, so she was away throughout much of the rapid rise in his swimming success.

* * *

DESPITE THE FACT THAT AARON STARTED GETTING A LOT OF PRESS after the move to Nova, Hayley was at the top of her game, too. She was turning in fast AA and AAA times, and qualified for the Junior Olympics— an indicator that her times ranked at the top of her age group in a regional context.[33] At first, she was small in stature, while lots of the competitive kids were on the tall side. In the world of swimming, it's well known that "the long boat travels faster." But Hayley was a speedy breaststroker. Under head coach Dave Salo, Nova was known as a "breaststroke factory," churning out the likes of Amanda Beard, Dave Denniston, Gabrielle Rose, and Jessica Hardy. And then, once Hayley was introduced to individual medley (called "IM," a race in which the swimmer completes all four competitive strokes), it became obvious that Hayley had incredible endurance.

"Little Hayley was nipping at the heels of Jeri Moss, who was *huge* by that time in freestyle, and we recognized there was something about Hayley's stamina," Wella remembers. "We were onto something. She's a distance swimmer."

Coach Brent Lorenzen helped Hayley develop her distance swims. She also topped out at a respectable five foot nine once she was in high school. Eventually, Hayley and Nova teammate Jeri Moss wound up together at Auburn.

Erin drew this poster to cheer on her sibling when Hayley qualified for Junior Olympics. COURTESY OF HAYLEY PEIRSOL

Despite the press that Aaron got, Hayley was one of the fastest girls coming up through the ranks at Nova.
PHOTO COURTESY OF HAYLEY PEIRSOL

"If her brother hadn't been Aaron Peirsol, she would have been recognized as one of the best young girls coming through the club" at Nova, Tim points out.

Lorenzen concurs. "Early on there were glimpses of that endurance, before I even started to coach her. The kids at eleven and twelve never swam longer than four hundred meters or five hundred yards. Within the program there hadn't been that emphasis yet. As she turned thirteen, fourteen, you could start to see her endurance. Then in high school, she made steady improvement. In 2000, at Junior Nationals, Hayley's goal was to make Trials. She just missed the Olympic team, but it was still a pretty big accomplishment."

"Hayley was blessed with this natural endurance and feel for the water," Lorenzen continues. "That, and her willingness to work and do whatever's asked of her, consistently. From home, from what I saw, there was support, encouragement, expectations, but Wella left the coaching to the coaches. I sort of want to describe Wella as having bigger-picture questions. She was good about supporting me as a coach."

"Hayley and I get along so well," Tim comments. "Everyone enjoys a little girl who's tougher than the boys. She was very endearing. Not spoiled, not a brat. She was super shy about some things, even painfully shy at a young age. But at the same time, she was the toughest physically and mentally, in the whole school. She just had to grow into herself, very similar to Wella."

He notes that there weren't the same sorts of activities available to girls when Wella was a teen, though an outlet like sports would have greatly benefited an active young woman such as her.

"And now," he says, of the shift toward girls in sports, "all those parents are thinking 'scholarship' since it's so expensive to go to college. We saw a lot of that. Ninety-nine percent of the parents are great people, just wondering, 'How far can we take our kid's talent?'"

At a serious age-group meet, the intensity of competition is evident. Even the youngest of competitors who swim fast draw speculation about potential. For parents who tend to live vicariously through their kids, the fun evaporates quickly. They coach their children right up to the ready bench, yell aggressively from the stands. Team parents sport some serious gear, promoting their kids and the team; even summer leagues print team visors, towels, and T-shirts. Promising kids receive private coaching, on top of the skills they garner from their club coach. However, Wella says they never could afford private coaches, except for one or two special occasions.

For Wella and Tim, Aaron's and Hayley's success in the pool led to complicated relationships with the other parents.

"We're the parents whose kid was usually successful, next to parents whose kid couldn't make the final," Wella says. "We told ourselves we couldn't be jumping up and down for Aaron and Hayley; it would be bad form. So we couldn't do right: We weren't jumping up and down for our kids, but we *couldn't* because they were always winning. Unfortunately, people saw us as snobby because we seemed withdrawn."

Complicating matters further was the prevalent prosperity in Orange County. As Tim expresses it, "If they could buy success, these kids would. So many could buy what they wanted, buy influence. But you can't buy success."

"You do dream bigger than what you wanted for yourself," Wella says, of what parents imagine for their children.

"When Aaron autographed," Tim interjects, "he used to sign 'Dream Big.' That's the cocoon he was in. We gave him everything he needed without the pressure."

Wella agrees: "To say what *you* want only makes them feel they've disappointed you."

"I can't make an Olympian," she concludes, "but I can make someone believe in themselves."

Chapter Seven : Responsibility

Wella's Tip for Staying Afloat: *If you want to raise great people, they have to be able to handle defeat. People have to teach kids they're not always going to win, and to lose gracefully.*

IT WAS BEGINNING TO SEEM TO WELLA THAT HER DREAMS for Aaron and Hayley might come true. At the same time, the family was facing some serious economic troubles that made the going rough for Wella and Tim. Even with their pooled resources, it was expensive to keep the kids in the swim programs. Besides the club fees for all four, they had to pay for each race in every meet that the kids entered.

However, Wella *knew* she was doing the right thing for the children by keeping them active and focused on their sport. She remembered how she had drifted without that kind of discipline and felt sure that this was the kind of structure Aaron and Hayley needed to channel their extraordinary energy. Plus, it was becoming clear they had abundant natural ability.

But just as Aaron began making waves in the swimming world, Wella found herself in real hot water. Money had always been tight, and while she had been living with her kids at her parents' house, she recalls turning her paycheck over every two weeks as her rent, though her dad occasionally gave her some money back.

Because she was only working part time, Wella still qualified for welfare, which helped her pay the bills and covered the childrens' health insurance. She tucked the pay stubs from her dental assistant job into an envelope that she mailed to the welfare office each month to report her income. When she inadvertently left out a pay stub once, she realized the result was a bigger welfare check.

So to stretch the dollars she received, she began leaving out one of her pay stubs each time she sent in her welfare report. She justified the dishonesty to herself: She needed the money for the kids, and she subscribed to the notion that she wasn't really hurting anyone. No one seemed to be paying attention to the small amount of extra money she netted from that deception.

Wella never breathed a word to anyone about what she was doing. She let things ride for two years, while life went on. When she and her kids eventually left her parents' house and moved into Tim's, the welfare office made so many inquiries about the address change that Wella worried they would audit her records. She stopped withholding pay stubs.

One day, near the end of the summer of 1994[34], Fran, who was suffering from brain cancer by that time, handed Wella a business card from two men who had come to the house during the day. Wella froze, suddenly tingling with ice-cold fear. She knew the gig was up. The card was imprinted with the words "Welfare Fraud Investigator," along with an agent's name and the address, phone number, and logo of the Orange County District Attorney's Office. On the back, a handwritten note read "Please contact us immediately."[35] Wella confessed her crime to Tim that night.

"I think they changed the wording [on the investigator's business card] not long after, because a lot of people would have skipped town if they had gotten that card," quips Wella sardonically. "Needless to say, I didn't sleep that night and called the welfare office at eight o'clock the next morning. They told me they wanted to meet with me. We immediately found an attorney, and Tim gave him a $1,500 retainer fee. We didn't have much, but he would have died for me.

"Tim didn't even belong in this," Wella says. Yet he stood by her.

Documents dated July 13, 1994, show that a criminal complaint had been filed, indicting Mary Louella Peirsol of felony public assistance fraud, stating that she "willfully, unlawfully and feloniously, by means of false statement and representation and by impersonation and other fraudulent device, obtain [sic] aid from Orange County for a child not in fact entitled thereto, food stamps, and medical assistance from Orange County" dating from August 1991 to about February 1994. An arrest warrant was issued and signed by Ron Stein, Investigator, who was named as the registered complainant, and Deputy District Attorney Aleta Bryant of Orange County.[36]

Legs folded under her in a chair, a tissue squeezed in her fist, Wella ventures to explain. She hasn't recounted this story to anyone. Only Tim, her parents, and siblings knew; she and Tim went out of their way to keep it from the children.

"When I had to meet with them at the welfare bureau, I was this young, tan mom. I don't think in a million years they thought they'd see a thing like me, with these two kids, either," she begins, referencing the recognition Aaron and Hayley were beginning to receive for their swim successes.

Wella first had to appear for a felony arraignment, where she was charged in front of Judge Craig Robison in the Municipal Court of Orange County, Harbor Judicial District, on August 18, 1994.[37] It was her thirty-seventh birthday.

Her case went to trial a month later, on September 22. Wella entered a guilty plea, accepting responsibility for her crime.

She waived her right to a jury trial, allowing her fate to rest on the discussion among the judge; her attorney, Michael Doudna; and the prosecutors. Recognizing the judge as someone she had seen around Newport Beach only deepened her humiliation. In court that day, Wella signed the guilty plea, which required her to accept a series of daunting clauses. The plea rendered her ineligible for probation, waived her rights to confront opposing witnesses or to appeal her case, and threatened deportation as a possible consequence for non-citizens[38]—a concern, as she had been born in Nova Scotia.

After an initial indictment, where formal charges were announced before the court, she and Tim waited nervously in the hallway outside the courtroom. When the attorneys finally came out, Wella remembers seeing only the backside of the prosecutor walking briskly away, hair swinging.

"The fact is that the district attorney was young and aggressive, and I had seen how she walked away. Our attorney didn't want to scare me until it was all over and we were sitting outside, but the DA—she was actually a deputy district attorney—was asking for prison time, *for jail!*" Wella emphasizes. Bryant had requested that Wella serve eighteen months to two years in prison for her crime.[39]

Luckily, the judge recognized something in her, perhaps her genuine remorse, Wella believes. Or maybe he considered the consequences for her children if their mother were to go to jail.

"The judge gave me four months of house arrest,"[40] she says, "and the DA was *fuming.*" There were already magazine articles about Aaron, so her attorney had brought those and showed the judge, asserting that this was not an irresponsible mother whose children should be taken from her.

"I've been told I'm a good mom, and I believe that I am, and that's the bottom line. It's kind of like an education: No one can take that away from you... even if I were in a jail cell." Wella falters and begins to cry. "It's beyond belief, if you love your children as much as I did. To have thought of leaving them—I can't even imagine.

"I could have had my kids taken away from me, and that frightened me a lot. There were a lot of things that kept me awake at night. Certainly nothing in my life has been as trying as that."

That afternoon, in lieu of jail time, the judge ordered that a monitor be locked around Wella's ankle for the next 120 days—officially noted in the records as "Home Electronic Confinement Monitored by Probation"—and required that she meet regularly with a probation officer for the next three years.[41]

"The penalty wasn't very stiff, was it, considering?" Wella reflects, thoughful. "The judge was pretty good to me. In fact, even my attorney was shocked that it was only going to be four months.

"After the trial was over, I had to go be booked," Wella remembers. She dressed in trendy white deck shoes, jeans, and a polo shirt and took the children to school.[42] Then she drove to Santa Ana, to report to the Central Justice Center by 9:00 a.m.

Looming over the sun-blanched streets a block or two from the neat town square in Santa Ana, the 1960s-era Central Justice Center seemed ominous and imposing, eleven stories high and built of industrial-looking steel scaffolding and grimy tinted glass. Though cigarettes are not the norm in health-conscious bastions of California, smokers clustered outside the courthouse, glaring through narrowed eyes at each passerby. Armed guards, bag scanners, and metal detectors controlled each entrance. Inside, everything seemed dirty white—walls, halls, old-style metal ice-tray fluorescent lighting, aging linoleum squares underfoot. Alert security officers scrutinized the crowd. Many people wore informal, inexpensive clothing and multiple tattoos; there was a long line at the "Criminal/Traffic" window. Briefcase-carrying lawyers moved in protective packs around the building.

"They fingerprinted me, and I had to do the picture and the whole nine yards," Wella recalls. "I didn't have to wear a jumpsuit, but they put me in a cell and shut it. I heard people screaming and yelling, saw inmates wearing jumpsuits, that kind of thing. And I remember thinking, *Oh my God*. I could be *staying* here. That's when it hit me."

The whole situation was especially incapacitating for someone used to taking life by the horns and *willing* things to go her way. Once the case started through the system, it didn't matter how determined she felt, because the results were completely out of her hands.

"So for four months, I ran around the backyard for my runs. I didn't swim for four months. I went to work every day, covered the ankle bracelet up with socks, and I made it through," she comments.

She paid back $17,000, the amount the welfare office said she owed. "They pad the numbers, so I had to pay more than I really took," she says, taking a deep, shuddering breath. "They add in their court time and expenses, so I had to pay that from the little money I was getting from the dentist's office. Obviously, I wasn't on welfare anymore. I paid back every single penny."

When the electronic probation ended, Wella had to reappear in court for the final hearing. On January 20, 1995, she came before the Honorable David O. Carter, to determine how much she would have to repay per month.[43]

"It was a different judge," Wella recalls. "He was looking over the file, and he said, 'Your son is Aaron Peirsol?' And I said, 'Yes, yes, he is.'" She cringed, hoping her mistake would not permanently be linked to her kids.

The kind judge told her she would have to pay $400 a month, when she was making about $500 a month. "He said, 'I know that's a lot for you to have to pay on your income. Maybe it can be brought down later.'

"He took my hand, he shook it, and he said, 'Good job,'" Wella remembers. "I turned around, looked at Tim, and started bawling."

For the next three years, she met regularly with the probation officer, producing stubs from her paychecks to verify her earnings. After two years, the $400 per month payment was lowered to $200 a month.

"It took me ten years to pay it off," she says.

All the while, she kept the secret from her children. Not feeling like she could share her shameful news with anyone, Wella felt even more isolated. Whenever the phone rang, she had to run and pick it up. She kept a three-prong phone they had to buy for that purpose in a back room they never used, and she would run in there to take the call. She had to hold the phone to the bracelet to prove that it wasn't just anybody answering.

She explained the circumstances to Dr. Millspaugh, and he kept her on at the office. "At work, a man would come in to make sure that I was there. He would sit in the lobby, and I would come up to the front, and he'd say, 'Are you Mary?' [in reference to her full given name, Mary Louella] and I'd say, 'Yes.' Then he'd say, 'Okay. See you later.' That was my probation. I was extremely lucky."

She continued working at that office until she decided to leave for a position with another dental office, right next to the high school. That office was so laid back, she doesn't even remember filling out a form to get the job; she avoided having to mention the felony on her record.

Though the penalty was far lighter than it could have been, it was effective: Instead of merely feeling slapped on the wrist, Wella experienced deep remorse that still haunts her.

"To be honest, I've always been afraid that if I tried to become an American citizen, they'd bring that up, and it's such a delicate subject for me," she notes, referring to her birth status as Canadian.

"I did what I thought I had to do to keep the kids swimming and keep my life going. That's the clincher, really, isn't it?" She pauses a few moments to regain her composure and wonders aloud how her children will react to the story she's telling.

"I think when they read it now, they'll probably cry for me because they know how badly I didn't want to hurt them. I made mistakes, too. Everybody does. But this could have been a really, really bad one.

It's huge. It's absolutely huge. I understand that."

The female probation officer was nice to Wella, and several times told her, "One day you'll look back at this, and, you know, you've got quite a story." Wella remembers thinking, *I don't* ever *want to tell this story.*

"But now that I've come to this place in my life, I realize, you know, *Top this one!* I've got these kids, these *amazing* kids. I made some big mistakes, and I also came from a pretty dysfunctional house—and I made it. If that's not inspiration for somebody, then I don't know what else to say."

"I dusted myself off, got up, and kept going," Wella concludes. "My kids never knew I'd have to drive to Santa Ana to meet with the welfare officer. They were too young to understand. They never even saw the bracelet. Good thing it wasn't summer, huh?"

Years later, the grown-up Aaron pauses, then smiles tightly. "I knew about that [bracelet]," he says quietly. "Oh, yeah. At the time, I didn't inquire. I know she probably tried to keep it from me, but there are only so many times you can stay home. I would have guessed it was about money, more than likely. They didn't really have any—there were four kids in the house, you know. And Tim was in the mortgage business, a very volatile business. My mom went to California with nothing on her back but us kids, and we got along. My mom did an incredible job."

Looking back on how the charge affected her life and her family, Wella notes, "I did not bring them into it. I did not want my children to have to live with my mistakes. That's exactly why—they were *my* mistakes, not theirs."

But Wella's trouble with the law and repaying her debt weren't the only financial waves the family had to face.

Tim's work in mortgage banking was often boom or bust.[44] Economists and public policy analysts agree that California was a "pivotal site of the bubble of the 2000s" and that California banks "engaged in some of the worst excesses of the housing bubble." Amid mass mortgage lending, ballooning home values, and sky-high housing costs, Californian homeowners were vulnerable, even in the years leading up to the crisis.[45] Irvine's median income ranked it among the richest cities in the United States, and its high cost of living reflected that affluence. Along with the rest of the state, the area was severely impacted by the audible pop as the housing bubble burst in the 1990s (as it would again, later, in 2009).[46]

Right about the time this economic roller coaster took a stomach-lurching plunge, Wella was paying restitution for her crime, and Tim was working in an industry that had crested the peak and was dropping full-speed into recession.

Not long after Wella's trial[47], she and Tim lost their home for financial reasons and rented a townhouse near the pool where Nova practiced. Never mentioning their fiscal troubles to the kids, they painted the switch as a way to simplify their lives.

"It was not a steady business, and we were lucky Tim saved for a rainy day. He had to reinvent himself," Wella says.

At one point, as Aaron was rocketing to prominence in the backstroke, the family didn't have the money to pay swim dues to Nova. Not wanting to worry the kids, Tim quietly went to talk to the board, a humiliating experience that still disturbs him, and asked them to allow him to put off the swim-team dues until he could get back on his feet financially.

"I guess people didn't want it to be easy for Wella and me," Tim remarks, noting he had served on the board himself for three years and felt he and Wella had been helpful and involved. "They kept asking, 'What are you doing for us?' when I already felt kicked down by having to ask."

"We've had our fair share of trouble, but the kids didn't know," Wella asserts. She did not want financial troubles to weigh on their self-esteem. "It was important for me not to let them know. I didn't want them to have to see what they didn't have. Aaron felt lucky to get to swim, and I wanted him to feel that way."

Chapter 8 : Talent

Wella's Tip for Staying Afloat: *You know when someone's so talented, but I couldn't have written this script.*

WHEN AARON TURNED THIRTEEN, COACH SALO PULLED HIM ASIDE. "I said, 'Look, I think you could make the Olympic team in the two hundred backstroke,'" relates Salo. Aaron, in his usual way, listened but never crowed about his coach's comment, not even to his parents.

"I identified what I thought he was capable of doing," Salo says. "He internalized it, which was to his credit. You knew it was in his head, but it wasn't vocalized. He wasn't talking down to other people.

"As a coach, it was an awesome experience to work with somebody so coachable. He was always receptive to what I had to say. He was okay with me having the vision and the plan; he didn't have to obsess about it."

As Aaron began to knock down age-group records, Wella noticed his habit of keeping track. In his Swim Guide, the comprehensive Southern California Swimming (SCS) record book that listed SCS and national age-group times, she saw that he had highlighted his race and penned, "in his own little handwriting," the time with which he broke the record.

"It was just the darlingest thing," she reminisces, with an indulgent smile.

Aaron was thinking about the big picture, even at that young age. As the grown-up Aaron commented to performance coach and blogger Doug Newburg, "The competition thing has always been interesting. It was never really about beating the guy next to me. It was more the process, doing it for myself. My bible when I was a kid was the record book. Each year a new one would come out and I remember when I was nine or ten, I would look through it and pick out the records I wanted to go after. It felt like the right way to go about it for me. Those times and records were my goals. People came and went along the way, but it was never a particular race or person. I was thinking beyond those guys."[48]

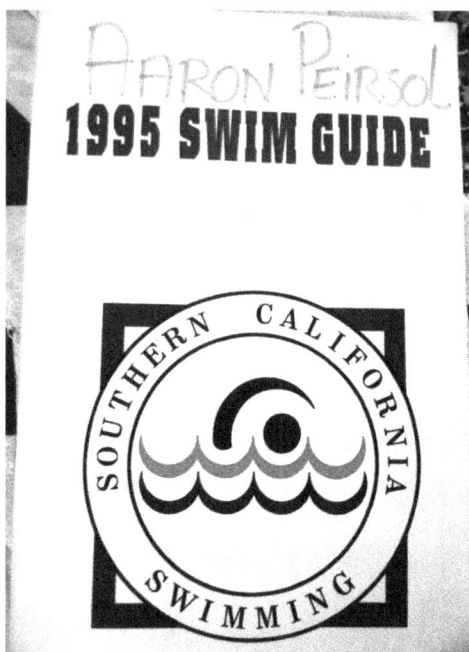

SOUTHERN CALIFORNIA AND NATIONAL AGE GROUP
11 - 12 BOYS
Short Course

SCS			NAG	
Christopher Pelant, UN	23.01 (89)	50 Yd. Freestyle	Ben Davidson, MS	22.63 (93)
Christopher Pelant, UN	50.60 (89)	100 Yd. Freestyle	Chas Morton, SE	49.46 (84)
Christopher Pelant, UN	1:50.43 (89)	200 Yd. Freestyle	Jeff McPherson, WT	1:47.72 (85)
John Edds, UN	4:55.81 (82)	500 Yd. Freestyle	Austin Lindsey, FL	4:47.96 (86)
Philippe Demers, MVN	26.81 (92)	50 Yd. Backstroke	David Chan, CC	25.32 (92)
Philippe Demers, MVN	58.52 (92)	100 Yd. Backstroke	David Chan, CC	54.79 (92)
AARON PEIRSOL	57.41 (95)			
David Katz, SCAL	29.27 (89)	50 Yd. Breaststroke	Chris Miller, MR	28.24 (94)
John Moffet, MT. BALDY	1:04.36 (77)	100 Yd. Breaststroke	Chris Miller, MR	1:00.84 (94)
Philippe Demers, MVN	24.59 (92)	50 Yd. Butterfly	Chas Morton, SE	24.50 (84)
Brian Alderman, SBSC	56.09 (82)	100 Yd. Butterfly	Chas Morton, SE	51.85 (84)
Raymond Papa, GLNY	58.02 (89)	100 Yd. Ind. Medley	David Chan, CC	55.93 (92)
Brian Alderman, SBSC	2:04.72 (82)	200 Yd. Ind. Medley		

BY AGE THIRTEEN, AARON WAS ALREADY SWIMMING against older competitors, finishing races with times faster than those expected of older age groups. Despite the growth of swim clubs nationally (with increasing numbers of swimmers), the sophistication of the athletes, and improved times (with faster pools and gear and better access to coaches), it is remarkable to compare current age-group times to those Aaron posted at his meets. As of this writing, Aaron's records in that 13–14 age group still stand—phenomenal, considering that it's been more than fifteen years.[49]

At the end of each swim season, Southern California Swimming held a banquet celebrating its top sixteen swimmers. On April 13, 1997, the keynote speaker for that banquet was Brad Bridgewater, gold medalist in the 200-meter backstroke event at the 1996 Olympics. Hayley saved a program from that banquet, autographed by Bridgewater: "To Hayley & Aaron, Swim Fast!"[50]

About two years later, reporter Erik Hamilton wrote in a newspaper article that twenty-six-year-old Bridgewater "was pushed to the limit Friday by Newport Harbor High sophomore Aaron Peirsol" at the Swim Meet of Champions in Mission Viejo. Bridgewater swam the race in 2:01.13; Aaron finished in 2:01.98, not quite a whole second behind.[51] Aaron was, at fifteen, close to out-touching a world-class athlete with a decade more experience, one who had already proven his mettle under pressure at the Olympics—an astonishing feat. Eventually, Aaron would edge Bridgewater out of a spot on the US Olympic team.

Although Aaron had not spoken to Wella and Tim about it, Coach Salo had set a series of goals for Aaron, all of which Aaron had conquered. Both swimmer and coach now felt sure that Aaron was going to the Olympics. About a year later, Coach Salo would ask for a meeting with Wella and Tim.

"'This is what we're planning,'" Tim says, paraphrasing Salo's words. "'We believe Aaron will be able to make the Olympic team in 2000.'

"At home, there had been no talk of the Olympics. We didn't know what it would take. For Wella and me, it seemed like all this just happened. Everything Dave told Aaron to do, he was doing" to get ready for Olympic Trials. Salo suggests that he didn't need to talk to the parents earlier. "I've done the same thing with Aaron as I did with Amanda Beard. How to prepare parents? *Don't change anything to change your life—do what you do.* I didn't have that conversation with Wella, because we had four years of development before the Olympics."

Coach Salo didn't want to worry Wella, because how would that help

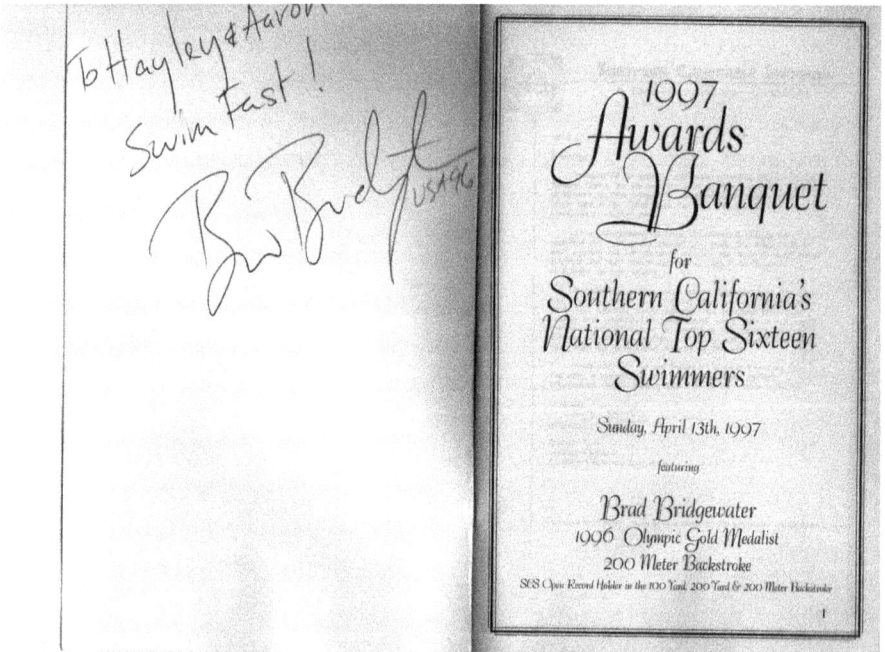

TOP: *Hayley apparently kept track in the Swim Guide, as well.*
PHOTO: LAURA COTTAM SAJBEL
BOTTOM: *Gold medalist Brad Bridgewater signed Hayley's and Aaron's program at the 1997 awards banquet, only two years before Aaron would beat him out of a spot on the Olympic team.* COURTESY OF HAYLEY PEIRSOL

Aaron?

So what is it that distinguishes the kid who has what it takes to make it to the Olympics? Salo believes coaches develop a knack for recognizing that special spark, and says that in his career he's only seen a "handful" of age-group swimmers with the whole package. In practice, and in races, he notes certain traits, particular swimmers who are "very coachable, very competitive," and consistent: "Every time they stepped up to the blocks to race, you had a sense of confidence that they were going to swim fast."

"Aaron has been a unique individual," Tim reflects. "Either he truly understood far beyond his years or he could just handle all that pressure. We never talked about his sets, how he did that. So the kids never felt a push other than to do their best."

Tim reiterates that he and Wella just "strapped in" to see what would happen, and that every day when they ran, Wella would confide in him her hope that Aaron would make the Olympics one day.

Tim was more grounded. He had been watching and analyzing sports all his life: "I used to think Aaron had a shot at being special, but I wondered, Is he going to be good enough? Have the drive? Prodigies in their sport are just wired for it, regardless of some parenting. Whatever it is, you can't pick it out in a crowd, normally. But Aaron, ever since he was a little guy, was so confident in his own skin."

* * *

IN THE SUMMER OF 1997, THIRTEEN-YEAR-OLD AARON went with the team to Clovis—a small town near Fresno, California, with a beautiful, Olympic-size outdoor swim facility—for his first Junior Nationals meet, where he won the 200-meter backstroke. Wella and Tim couldn't attend this meet. They both had to work, Wella was still on probation, and they had Hayley at home. Brian Pajer, who was assisting Coach Salo at the meet, gave them the play-by-play of Aaron's race over the phone.

The next year, in 1998, Aaron returned to Clovis, but by then his times qualified him to swim at Nationals with the "big boys," swimmers who were the best in the United States. Wella, Tim, and Hayley came up to watch this meet, making a day trip. Wella remembers wandering over to the area where the swimmers were cordoned off from the crowd and spotting individual-medley greats Tom Dolan (1996 and 2000 Olympics) and Eric Namesnik (1992 and 1996 Olympics) milling around inside. When she finally spotted

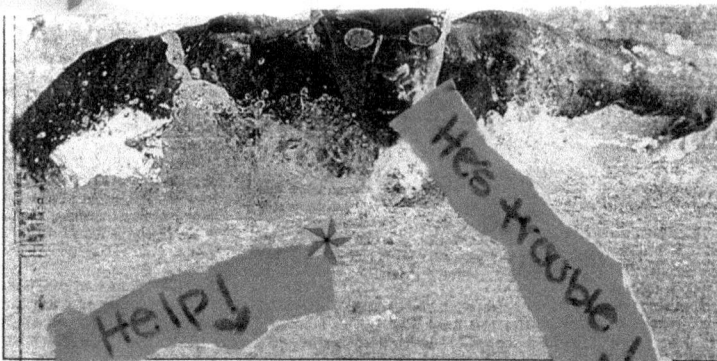

Watch out for AARON!

He's trouble!

Help!

GLENN KO...   ...eles Times

Juan Velo... of the Mission Viejo Nadadores wins the 200 butterfly in a time of 2 minutes 2.06 seconds.

Bridgewater in Troubled Waters

■ Swimming: Newport Harbor's Peirsol puts some pressure on 1996 Olympic gold medalist.

By ERIK HAMILTON
TIMES STAFF WRITER

It appears Brad Bridgewater doesn't quite have a watertight hold on a U.S. Olympic team spot.

Bridgewater, a 1996 Olympic gold-medal winner, was pushed to the limit Friday by Newport Harbor High sophomore Aaron Peirsol in the 200-meter backstroke at the Swim Meet of Champions in Mission Viejo.

Bridgewater, 26, ranked second in the world, clocked the fastest preliminary time Friday morning with a 2 minute 04.80 second swim at the Marguerite Swim Complex. But Peirsol, 15, ranked fourth in the world, was only 16 one-hundredths of a second behind him.

Lenny Krazelburg, Bridgewater's teammate on the Trojan Swim Club, is ranked first in the world but is not competing in Mission Viejo.

Bridgewater and Peirsol were neck and neck until the last 50 meters, when Peirsol's turn was not

as sharp as Bridgewater's. That turn was the difference, as Bridgewater finished in 2:01.13. Peirsol finished second in 2:01.98.

As the Olympic trials get closer, it has become apparent that Bridgewater and Peirsol will be strong contenders for a spot on the U.S. Olympic team. Only the top two swimmers in an event qualify for the team and Krazelburg is expected to be the top qualifier in the event.

"In the last couple of years I've had a good comfort zone hanging out in the top one and two in the world and not having to worry about anybody else," Bridgewater said. "With Aaron here, it gives me more of a sense of urgency."

Peirsol, who said he was more tired and hungry than disappointed with his second-place finish, said he still has time to work on his stroke and correct the mistakes before next year. Anyway, he likes being in the chase mode.

"I would much rather be chasing someone than have someone chasing me," Peirsol said. "It's more exciting. I'm very happy with that time, especially since I've been working out hard. It's the fastest time for me this season."

In other men's events, Jason Lezak of the Irvine Novaquatics

held off Bart Kizierowski of the Mission Viejo Nadadores to win the 100 freestyle in 51.18. Kizierowski, the former Mission Viejo High standout, finished in 51.23.

The Nadadores' Chad Carvin won his second event, clocking a 3:55.96 in the 400 freestyle. Juan Veloz, Carvin's teammate, won the 200 butterfly (2:02.06).

Former Olympian Ashyley Tappin of the Novaquatics won the 100 freestyle in 57.81.

Kaitlin Sandeno, a sophomore at El Toro High who swims for Nellie Gail Swim Club, added a 400 freestyle victory to Thursday's 800 win.

Sandeno won the event in 4:17.07. Sweden's Asa Sandlund of Mission Viejo was second (4:21.10). While Sandeno's finish in the 400 free was expected, her second-place finish Friday in the 200 butterfly was not.

Sandeno was defeated by Misty Hyman of Desert Fox. Hyman, who's the NCAA Division I champion, won in 2:11.20. Sandeno finished in 2:12.61.

"I found out a couple weeks ago at a Simi Valley meet that I'm not that bad in the fly," Sandeno said. "I hadn't done the stroke in so long, so when I did it two weeks ago and was only a second off the Olympic trial time, I said, 'Wow.'"

In a scrapbook she made for Aaron, Hayley personalized
the article about how Aaron nearly beat Bridgewater.
COURTESY OF HAYLEY PEIRSOL

him, Wella marveled that Aaron, at fourteen still just a kid, was standing among these swimming heavyweights.

"I mention Tom Dolan, because I was *in awe*," she emphasizes, her voice cracking, still enthralled by the memory. "They have the swimmers in a place surrounded by gates. Tom Dolan's parents were over there waiting, too, and I remember thinking, There's Tom Dolan! Oh my God, that's so cool! Aaron is standing right next to him!" Dolan was tall and lanky at six foot seven; Aaron's lean, six-foot-three frame looked small in comparison.

There were qualifying heats—a C flight, a B flight, then the A final (the "Damn Fast," as Tim calls that last one)—pitting Aaron against the best in the world at that time, Lenny Krayzelburg and Brad Bridgewater. Aaron was in an outside lane, meaning he was seeded to finish seventh or eighth, but he took third. Wella and Tim had had no expectations before this race of where Aaron fit in to the big picture. However, as the finish times went up on the board, someone nearby commented memorably, "Aaron kind of skipped through Senior Nationals to Pan Ams."

Wella turned to ask, "What are Pan Ams?"

* * *

THE PAN AMERICAN GAMES ARE A FESTIVAL OF ALL SPORTS—from archery to wrestling—among competitors from all nations in the Americas. It is held every four years, scheduled for the year prior to each summer Olympics. Wella and Tim soon learned that the first- and second-place finishers at the US National Championships qualify for World Championships (held the year prior to the Olympic Games); third- and fourth-place finishers qualify for the Pan American Games; and the fifth and six-place finishers head to the World University Games. Aaron went to Pan Ams in 1999; it was his first international meet.

Looking back, Wella recognizes that "Clovis was the defining moment. At Nationals, in the summer of 1998, Aaron made the Pan Ams, swimming with Lenny Krayzelburg. He leapfrogged from Junior National times to National times and made the US swim team."

In a high school scrapbook that Hayley made for Aaron is the original letter from USA Swimming, dated the following April 29, 1999, officially inviting Aaron to be on the US swim team after he placed at Nationals. Being a member of the team qualified him for a stipend and health insurance—both were of huge financial help to the family—and ensured that Aaron would be trained to help the United States face "a more formidable challenge than ever before from our foreign competition in preparation for the 2000 Games." Wella and Tim flew into Winnipeg in the summer of 1999 for Pan Ams, on a hop from Minneapolis in a plane they describe as "a 1940s warplane." On the flight, they met a young woman traveling with her baby, and she offered to have her husband drive them to the hotel. The couple drove Wella and Tim past their own home and gave them a tour of the town before delivering them to the hotel.

But Winnipeg was not nearly the romantic place Wella had imagined it to be. The natatorium was quite a ways out of the city center, though forty Western Hemisphere nations were in attendance.[52] Wella was shocked to unexpectedly see Scott Peirsol and his father in the stands and felt a surge of protectiveness for Aaron. It chilled her to see Scott and know that his presence might upset Aaron at such a critical time. Aaron and Hayley had not seen their father since their long-ago visit to Florida in 1992. Wella shivered and worried as she watched Scott, who waited until Aaron finished his race to go down to talk.

As with most surprises, Aaron took Scott's appearance in stride. "He came to a few of my meets," Aaron recalls later. "I must say it never affected me negatively. He was just showing up and watching, always being very respectful. I wasn't really in communication with him, but it never startled me to see him. He is my father, and I figured I'd see him here and there. But he never asked for anything in return. I never feared that; he never crossed a line with me."

The athletes from all the different countries stayed together in a "village—actually the grounds of a local college fenced off from the public—to simulate the experience created for athletes at the Olympics.

"We tried to go see Aaron, but we couldn't get in. Finally, someone found him. He was clearly having fun and gave us this 'Why are you here?' attitude," Wella recalls, laughing at the sentiment so typical of a teenager.

Aaron, as usual, seemed as self-possessed as possible in making the jump into such an overwhelming venue. He took silver in the 200-meter backstroke, right behind Leonardo Costa of Brazil, a twenty-six-year-old. Aaron was fifteen.

"They raise the flags for the winners, and that was the first time they raised the American flag for Aaron," Tim recalls. Before Winnipeg, Aaron had been considered "up and coming," but Tim and Wella describe life since then as a blur of memories, something they couldn't have even dreamed—"although Wella *did* dream it," Tim points out.

*Aaron's photo flashed on the screen at Pan Ams
in Winnipeg, after he took silver in 1999.*
PHOTO COURTESY OF WELLA HARTIG

"Growing up, I could not wait for the Olympics every four years, to hear all those stories behind the athletes," Tim says. "Since 2000, I haven't actually seen any Olympic coverage." Instead, he and Wella have been seated in person at the Olympic Games. "We've been all over the world, places we never would have traveled. What an incredible ride he's allowed us."

Chapter 9 : Perseverance

Wella's Tip for Staying Afloat: *"If you raise your children to feel that they can accomplish any goal or task they decide upon, you will have succeeded as a parent and you will have given your children the greatest of all blessings."* —Quotation by Brian Tracy,[53] the May entry on a calendar Hayley made as Wella's Christmas gift

GIVEN THEIR FINANCIAL CIRCUMSTANCES AS the 2000 Olympics approached, there seemed to be no way Wella and Tim could come up with the money to fly to and stay in Sydney, should Aaron make the Olympic team. Then their luck changed. That May, a friend of Wella's from the dentist's office, Michele Mullen, spearheaded a fundraiser for the family at Shark Island, now the Newport Beach Yacht Club[54], with invitations sent only to friends outside the swimming world, to avoid fanning any sensitive feelings among fellow swim families. John Moffet, a breaststroker from Stanford who had been named to two Olympic teams, in 1980 and 1984, spoke at the fundraiser on behalf of Aaron. People donated items for a silent auction; nearly 150 people attended. Michele recalls that the event raised several thousand dollars and involved help from Wella's sister Patte and several of the water polo families, whose kids were friends with Aaron.

At the time, the economy had dipped and lots of Californians were taking out second mortgages, a point Wella and Tim make to underscore the generosity of those who came to help. The fundraiser had to be held before Aaron officially made the team—the time was short between the Olympic Trials and the actual Games—but Coach Dave Salo felt so certain about the outcome that the event forged ahead.

One donor took Tim aside and offered his frequent-flyer miles to send the family to Sydney. Then, Wella and Tim got a call regarding "an anonymous person who wants to know if there's anything he can do." After Aaron officially made the team, that benefactor called again to ask, "What do you

A snapshot of Aaron at practice, when he was sixteen.
PHOTO COURTESY OF WELLA HARTIG

need to make the trip doable?"

"A check came in the mail from a foundation that we couldn't track and helped pull it together for us," remembers Wella. "You know, a lot of parents don't get to go, can't afford it. We've heard stories [at the Olympics], about how a whole town got together to send some parents. But for us, living in Southern California, some people were saying, 'They don't need that money. Look into them—they don't need the money.' People we thought were our friends weren't there helping."

Fortunately, others were. Wella's friend Barbara, a fellow Y lap-swimmer, had once been a flight attendant and remained in touch with a pilot and his family in Sydney, who graciously offered their home to Tim, Wella, and Hayley for the duration of the Olympics. Things appeared to be coming together.

It is not uncommon for parents of Olympians to be strapped for funds, after scrimping and saving for the training their prodigies require to ascend to the highest levels of sport. While spectators are thrilled by the prowess of the athletes, they tend to assume that someone covers expenses for these talented competitors, who practice single-mindedly for years to represent their country. Many athletes in unsponsored sports are reduced to fundraising through bingo games and bake sales, to cover basic expenses.[55]

After the Pan Ams in Winnipeg, family life changed for Wella, Tim, and the kids. "You're never the same once someone is that good," Wella observes. Events suddenly seemed to swirl around them, and there was no time to prepare. They were in for the ride of their lives, with almost no idea about what to expect.

"It was surreal," Wella remembers. "I was not even sure how the process worked—the Trials, making the team… I didn't even know the athletes went to camp. I don't even remember that swim when he made it in the two-hundred-meter backstroke."

* * *

THE OLYMPIC TRIALS TOOK PLACE IN AUGUST 2000 in Indianapolis. In the 100-meter backstroke event, Aaron, who had turned seventeen the previous month, took fourth place with a time of 56.15, behind nineteen-year-old Randall Bal and twenty-four-year-old Neil Walker. Lenny Krayzelburg, also twenty-four—who in 1999 had set the world record for the event with 53.60—punctuated his win with an Olympic Trial record of 53.67 seconds. However, the 200-meter backstroke was closer: Even though Krayzelburg set a second Olympic Trial record, with 1:57.31, Aaron finished right on his tail with a final time of 1:57.98.

Traditionally, the winner makes the US Olympic team, but there was some lingering uncertainty about who else would be selected, as more experienced swimmers like 1996 gold medalist Brad Bridgewater were still in the mix in Aaron's event.

"We had no expectations," Wella recalls. She was nervous, and could only pray that Aaron would make it. "No parent is *not* nervous, if their kid has a shot at going. There are a lot of guys that have come in third to Aaron who were more experienced. I think about those parents and how blessed we were, because he ultimately made three Olympic teams."

The official announcement was dramatic: After the meet, the swimmers were paraded onto a balcony overlooking the pool deck, and the 2000 Olympic team was named one at a time—including Aaron Peirsol, who had just completed his sophomore year of high school.

Wella, Tim, and Hayley squeezed into the press conference afterward to listen as Aaron was interviewed alongside several other athletes. It felt unreal to watch Aaron up on the podium, taking questions from the media, Wella recalls. When they left Indianapolis after the Trials, Aaron stayed behind with the Olympic team. Wella wasn't sure when he would be home; however, a few days later, he flew back to Orange County to pick up his passport and other necessities.

"Aaron never showed us that he was under pressure," Wella remembers, "but he was losing hair. His hair was coming out in chunks. I didn't want to say, but I knew right away that it was so much stress."

Aaron regards it differently. He says he felt all right at that point, even though his mother was worried. "Parents are not in the pool, not told what it's going to take," he explains. "I accept the consequences and risks, but those watching may not know the risks and what that means."

In other words, it might actually be more traumatic to watch your child from the bleachers than to put yourself on the line in the pool. At least in the water, your fate is somewhat in your own hands. Once the race is under way, an athlete does exactly what he (or she) has been training to do his entire life.

The day after Aaron returned from Indianapolis, the family drove him to Pasadena, two hours away, where he was to stay at the Olympic training camp with the other team members. The team was housed at a swanky hotel, so Wella and Tim checked Aaron in and accompanied him upstairs to his room. When they opened the door, the room was dark; at first, they didn't see the person sitting inside. Aaron, always practical, went to open the blinds, and there sat Michael Phelps, fifteen years old at the time, decked out in a suit and tie, sitting motionless on the bed as if he weren't sure what to do next. The family knew Michael, of course—elite swimming is a relatively small world—and Aaron's presence seemed to put Michael back in the moment. Aaron and Michael tore into the gift baskets placed for them in the room, a perk the more experienced athletes seemed to take in stride. Hit with the realization that these were really only boys, Wella had a hard time leaving them.

"When we shut the door on those two—Aaron was *just barely s*eventeen years old—there with all those twenty-two- and twenty-four-year-old *men*… Aaron and Michael were still just goofy kids, while the others were college guys," she remembers.

Since it wasn't far, Wella, Tim, and Hayley made the trip to Pasadena a couple of times over the next two weeks to check in—"Not that Aaron wanted to see us," Tim jokes, referring to the fact that Aaron was enjoying the camaraderie without parental oversight, "but we got to hear good stories." For example, Wella and Tim share an anecdote one of the coaches passed along to illustrate Aaron's remarkably relaxed and unpretentious nature.

The coaches were sitting around in the lobby once when Aaron walked past. Offhandedly, he nodded and said, "Hey, guys," to these legendary men, a self-confident gesture that reportedly impressed several of them.

The Olympic training camp was designed to help the athletes taper off from their peak performance, and to rebuild them in time for the Olympics, to be held in September that year, and to turn the loose alliance of athletes into a team.

"It's almost military," Wella explains. "They develop into a team, fit them for outfits. My best way of looking at it is you're serving your country. True Olympians act like Olympians. They represent their country. You get a medal for your country. It's like being in the military, in that it's regimented, uniformed. The athletes are told to act and speak a certain way. It starts young, too, but that is kept under wraps."

Coach Brian Pajer explains that youth camps are held annually to tutor some of the best age-group athletes. There, coaches selected from across the country teach their young charges to field questions from the media, train at altitude, and practice alongside other elite competitors, preparing them for the eventuality of making the national stage in their events.[56]

"Once his times got noticed, Aaron was always in camps," Wella explains. "They would go to Colorado Springs in the fall. All kinds of athletes go and stay in these bungalow-type rooms. One mom told me recently that her son found 'Aaron Peirsol '97' carved on a bed there."

Two weeks before the 2000 Olympics, Aaron and the athletes on the US team flew to Australia to acclimate, but they did not go directly to Sydney. They would get on a bus approximately a week before the Games and ride into Sydney together for their first glimpse of the Olympic Village and the sparkling, pristine pool where they would be racing.

"It's a big moment," Wella emphasizes, pausing for effect, "when they first get to look around and see."

No one trains in that pool until a week before the actual Olympic Games, when they are assigned official practice times.

Meanwhile, Wella, Tim, and Hayley prepared for their own grand adventure. On top of the excitement of the Olympics was the thrill of flying overseas to Australia. Tim recalls that the family got bulkhead seating for the trip from Los Angeles to Sydney, so they could prop their feet against the wall. He worked with Hayley on some math, as she had started her first week of school before leaving.

"It was really, really exciting, going ten thousand miles away, across the world. Neither of us had ever done that," Wella remembers. For someone born in Sydney, Nova Scotia, this Sydney was truly the other side of the globe. "Getting off the plane, it really *felt* like you were 'down under.' People went out of their way for us—without even knowing who we were. Americans were really well liked at that time, before the war [in Iraq and Afghanistan]. We were elated. Even Hayley, who was fifteen and not generally thrilled about hanging out with her parents, was happy to be there with us. It was such a massive thing. Until Aaron had his very first swim, I don't think it sunk in."

Their host met them at the airport and whisked them to his home, where his wife and three children (twin girls and another daughter) greeted them warmly. "We felt a little like aliens; although we all spoke English, the different way words were used became amusing," Tim says. "Later in the visit, when we asked the children to 'root' for Aaron, we were told that 'root,' down under, referred to sexual activity… oops!" Their host family put together a barbeque that night with the next-door neighbors—who happened to be relatives with twin boys and a daughter.

Within an hour of arriving at their hosts' home, Wella and Tim ferreted out the nearest public swimming pool and were able to get their usual workout to shake some of the jet lag before the welcome barbeque. It turned out that the pool they found was the "home" pool of Aussie sensation Ian Thorpe. (They would continue this practice of finding pools for their workouts all over the world in their future travels following Aaron and Hayley, with the only exception being Beijing.)

The next day, they took a run through the neighborhood and swam again. They left Hayley at the house with the twin girls, who were a year younger and charmed by having an American in their midst. Hayley talked the girls into letting her dress them up and when Wella and Tim returned, the girls were wildly painted in lipstick with crazy hairdos. Fun-loving Hayley was hiding, giggling and refusing to let the girls return the "favor."

Later that day, they ventured into Sydney proper, catching a train at the nearby station and navigating into the heart of downtown, by the harbor. Thousands of people from all over the world milled about the streets, trading and buying Olympic pins, and Tim notes, "It seemed like Disneyland in that way." Downtown, banners sporting enormous photos of swimmers billowed from the buildings. In the States, Wella points out, the popular athletes would be basketball or football players, but the national sports stars in Australia were the swimmers.

"The buses were even wrapped in swimmers," she exclaims, referring to the marketing practice of completely covering city buses in a skin of advertising.

They were wowed by the over-the-top architecture near the harbor and the soaring Sydney Opera House. They marveled at the flags draped over buildings where other countries' athletes were housed. "For example, you'd see the Swiss flag and know the Swiss athletes were staying there," Wella clarifies. "All the countries had their own little gathering spots. The US had a prime spot, a family center sponsored by AT&T, where parents and relatives of American athletes could enjoy free food and drink as well as free phone calls back to the US.

"That was like a marketplace, with refrigerated shelves of yogurt, drinks—just there for the taking!" she exclaims.

Over the course of their visit, she, Tim, and Hayley would spend quite a bit of time at the center, as it both saved money and exposed them to families of athletes from all sports, not just swimming.

"Towards the end of swimming, there was a changing of the guard: Track and field started, and the makeup of the crowd there changed," Wella remembers. "We realized it had been our own little world—the swimmers were 'ours'—and it was time to move on. Things got louder, and we realized there were different personalities in different sports."

As this was Aaron's first experience at the Olympics, the family had no expectations; there was not too much pressure riding on Aaron's performance. "I was just hoping he would place," Wella says. And because swimming is enormously popular in Australia, it was a lot of fun for a family involved in that sport.

"We had no idea of what swimming was in Australia. No one told us how into swimming and sports the Aussies are. Once we got inside the natatorium, people were yelling, 'Aussie! Aussie! Aussie!' and then would be the echo—'Oy! Oy! Oy!'—across the stands. We had never seen this [rowdy enthusiasm] before at swim meets. And it's such a clean sport usually, but there was *alcohol* served! That never goes on at swim meets that we'd been to," she observes.

Never before having been in the midst of such prestigious competition, Wella and Tim tried to take things a step at a time. They didn't feel especially nervous, although Tim says he did think Aaron had a real chance for gold, as "his improvement curve was off the charts." US teammate Lenny Krayzelburg was favored to win and had already taken gold in the 100-meter

TOP *Jamie Rauch, Aaron, and Nate Dusing struck a pose in their Ralph Lauren–designed USA Olympic team jackets, at the opening ceremonies in Sydney.*
BOTTOM: *Wella took this photo from her seat near the rafters of the Sydney Olympic Park Aquatic Centre: Aaron (at left) on the Jumbotron. In the bottom corner of the photo is a glimpse of the pool, far down below.*
PHOTOS COURTESY OF WELLA HARTIG

backstroke event before Aaron's part of the competition began. The format was different than any the family had previously experienced—with morning preliminaries, semi-finals for the top sixteen the same night, and finals for the top eight the following evening.

"In the morning, he swam and made the top sixteen. I felt good because he didn't look stressed," Wella remarks, thinking back. During the preliminary races, the Australian hosts brought in school children in their uniforms to fill up the stands. In the evening, for the semi-finals, more people started to arrive. "The night of the finals, it was packed to the hilt!" Wella exclaims. "The circle seeding put him in heats so that the top four don't swim against each other until the final. I was probably scared to death about the final, but he had nothing to lose. I just prayed he would medal, under pressure." Although Michael Phelps had also made the team, he did not medal at the 2000 Olympics.

The Sydney Olympic Park Aquatic Centre is enormous and modern, with slick amenities like underwater viewing windows alongside the competition pool. Built as a showcase by the young Triple 'M' Group as part of Sydney's Olympic bid, the ten-lane competition pool stretches 50 meters long, with a moveable bulkhead. Soaring, arched beams, glass, and steel form the ceiling; and stands elevated above the press-box seats lend the place the feel of an echoing airplane hangar. For the Olympics, seating was boosted to hold a crowd of seventeen thousand.[57]

Tim and Wella didn't like the way the stands were set up. The parents of the American Olympians were seated "way up in the nosebleed section," Wella recalls. "Aaron looked like a pea on the deck from our seats. We could only see him on the Jumbotron."

So they watched. Wella imagines what it must have been like, when Aaron walked on deck and looked out at a stadium where every seat was taken. "It must have been intimidating," she reflects. "The only other international meet he'd been to was Pan Ams, not nearly this size. At the Olympics, everyone was from other countries, coaches speaking in different languages, lots of high security—it was completely different. Ian Thorpe, this was his country, and he had all that support. He was *lucky!* But I think Aaron was overwhelmed. He didn't expect that many people to be there."

Sitting next to Wella was the mother of another American swimmer, who cheered for Lenny Krayzelburg in the race against Aaron, though she realized Aaron was Wella's son. "That was my first introduction to being there," Wella says. "If it were me next to a first-time mother of an Olympian,

TOP *Hayley, fifteen, and Wella, at the Olympics in Sydney* LEFT *Aaron, towel over head, walks onto the deck before his first ever Olympic race.* PHOTOS COURTESY OF WELLA HARTIG

I would have grabbed that person's hand and said, 'I know what you're going through.'"

Tim recounts the race the family had come so far to watch: "At that stage in his career Aaron would be behind until the last wall and then just mow people down in the last fifty meters. So the race seemed familiar in that way, but he just couldn't catch Lenny." However, Aaron gave an amazing performance.

Krayzelburg hit the wall first, in 1:56.76, Aaron not quite a second behind at 1:57.35. Aussie Matthew Welsh touched a quarter of a second later for third, in 1:57.59.

Aaron had won a silver medal. The family was absolutely thrilled.

Because they were aching to see Aaron in person after such a huge win, Wella, Tim, and Hayley waited three hours—the time it took for Aaron to complete a required drug test before he was allowed to leave the natatorium.

After that long wait, they got to hug and congratulate Aaron. They were all elated to be there, sharing his success. Finally, Tim, Wella, and Hayley took the train an hour back to the home where they were staying, exhausted. Arriving well after midnight, they were surprised and delighted to find the front door decorated with an aluminum foil silver medal and a sign that read "Good on ya, Aaron!"

The last few days in Sydney, the pressure was off, and Tim, Wella, and Hayley toured the Sydney Zoo and some other landmarks. Word filtered through that Aaron wanted to get together, so they planned a harbor cruise for the family. Just as they were to board, the crew announced that there would be a significant delay; a passenger on a previous cruise had slipped and broken a leg. Since Aaron didn't have much time to spare, they returned to the AT&T Center, "where," Tim says good-naturedly, "we found out why Aaron really wanted to see us."

It turned out that *Sports Illustrated* was hosting a yacht party in the harbor that night, but underage Aaron needed parental permission to go and to stay out past the 10:00 p.m. curfew. Wella and Tim thought this inappropriate, considering how young Aaron was, and refused to let him attend. "He left pretty quickly as he 'had to get back,'" Tim jokes, "code for 'you guys are really ruining my trip.' I'm not sure he ever forgave us."

Back in the States, the family—including Wella's mother, Patte, Joey, and the cousins—eagerly awaited Aaron's flight and picked him up at Los Angeles International Airport. He arrived on a plane with many other Olympians, including Venus Williams. Wella's friend Michele sparked the idea that Newport Beach should hold a parade for Aaron. She and Patte worked with the

Aaron, Hayley, and Greg, who was in town for a visit, after the Sydney Olympics. PHOTO COURTESY OF WELLA HARTIG

American Legion to solicit the first-ever parade permit for Newport Beach. They drove the potential route to see how long it would be, and rustled up council members, a band, and Girl Scouts to participate.[58]

"It actually came to pass," Tim says. "I'm not sure they've had a parade since. But through a lot of volunteer effort, it turned out really well and, looking back, it was amazing it ever happened."

On Friday, December 1, 2000, the *Daily Pilot* reported that the city of Newport Beach "issued a rare parade permit for Olympic swimming silver medalist Aaron Peirsol." The following Saturday, officially renamed Aaron Peirsol Day, authorities cleared the Balboa Peninsula to make way for the festivities honoring the seventeen-year-old:

> Leading the proud parade pack will be the Newport Harbor band, followed by the day's namesake riding in a vintage 1910 Rambler convertible.

> "It'll be cool to see who's there," Peirsol said.

> For starters there will be a Newport Beach Fire Department truck, followed by such local dignitaries as City Council members.... Two troupes of Girl Scouts... followed by their younger counterparts, the Brownies, who will travel via Razor scooters.

And bringing up the rear will be Peirsol's aquatic buddies, the Newport Harbor High's CIF Southern Section Division I championship waterpolo team. The recently victorious team will, like Peirsol, be carried in a motorcade of vintage cars. The parade will begin at the Balboa Pier and end with a barbecue bash at the American Legion Hall, 215 15th St.[59]

"The Olympics in Sydney were just magical," Wella says. "That silver medal was *gold* for Aaron—in front of eighteen thousand people. No one thought he or Michael [Phelps] would medal. It was only Aaron's second international meet."

After all the fanfare, carrying the mantle of awe-inspiring Olympian and silver medalist, Aaron had to shake off the jet lag and begin his junior year of high school.

As for Wella, she had turned around a lifetime of disappointment.

Chapter 10 : Intensity

Wella's Tips for Staying Afloat: A sports hero has to grow up like any other kid—or else something will go wrong later.

THE FAMILY TRIED TO GET BACK TO NORMAL AFTER SYDNEY, as Aaron and Hayley finished up at Newport Beach High School, taking classes and swimming for the NBHS Sailors as well as for Nova. But for Wella, the pressure of Aaron's suddenly soaring fame began to take a toll.

Reporters and fans wanted to know what he ate for breakfast, his vital stats, every tiny detail of the family's lives. Aaron had to make appearances, give interviews, and, even more than before, was required to fly around the country on his own, when he was still only a junior in high school. There were new levels of pressure to consider potential college teams or professional contracts for endorsements. Wella's natural protectiveness went into overdrive, yet there was no way to stem the endless demands. Even her intense exercise routine wasn't enough to quell the unease of the insatiable public scrutiny.

"Aaron handled it amazingly well, but I was completely unprepared," Wella says.

Added to that pressure was the stress of sending the children off to college. Trying to keep all the kids focused on issues beyond winning in the pool, Tim and Wella had been building the groundwork for what they hoped would pay off long-term in a broader education. Though neither of them had left home for college, they felt strongly about the importance of getting the kids to consider universities away from Southern California, to have new experiences in the world.

"In our house, there was no other thought process than going off to college," Tim states.

"We were big on that," Wella confirms. "I had the opportunity to go but didn't take it."

"And I drove thirty-five to forty minutes a day to finish college," Tim says. "We both knew the way we did it isn't the way to get it done. You need to go away. The growth from that experience is immense."

Tim illustrates his point with the example of a nephew who left his hometown to attend Loyola Marymount University in Los Angeles: "He went in still a kid and crewed [on the rowing team] for four years. Now that young man is physically fit, looks you in the eye. He got away from his comfort zone." In contrast, he says he and Wella were both the youngest in their own families and had been reluctant to leave familiar surroundings. "You try to do so much for your kids, but lowering expectations doesn't produce interesting people—real people."

Knowing what you should do is easier than actually sending your children out into the world to fend for themselves. Even though she knew they were doing the right thing, it wasn't easy for Wella when the Aaron left home to attend college at the University of Texas in Austin, almost 1,400 miles away.

Anxiety, the unhealthy side of intensity, had been plaguing her as Aaron's fame grew. As close as she felt to her kids, his absence was a real struggle for her.

Wella, whom Tim calls a "worrier," hit the wall one morning. Driving Hayley to high school, she suddenly felt her heart pumping so hard she could barely breathe. Her vision blurred, and her focus narrowed. She was in traffic and didn't know what was wrong or what to do. Somehow she made it to the campus and dropped Hayley off before calling her sister Patte.

Patte took Wella to see an internist who prescribed some herbs and vitamins to soothe her anxiety. Wella, Tim, and Aaron were scheduled to fly to the Bahamas for a photo shoot that night, and the doctor told Wella she would be fine to fly. Though it was work for Aaron, the trip was supposed to be a treat for the three of them, a bit of respite from all the craziness. However, once she was on the plane, Wella (who hates to fly) fell apart again, and the medics were waiting for her as she de-boarded the plane in Miami. Aaron was obligated to catch the connecting flight to the Bahamas, so he stayed at the airport. Tim went with Wella in the ambulance to what Wella, literally in a state of panic, thought was "the Frankenstein hospital," where nurses kept speaking Spanish to her, miring her frightening medical experience in even more confusion.

"Then *Boris Karloff* came in—Tim will tell you!" she exaggerates, ridiculing her own fears. "And he was taking me to this huge… *chamber-like thing* to do an MRI of my brain. *I'm dying here,"* she remembers thinking, then laughs at the absurdity of it all.

An IV with some Darvocet alleviated the symptoms, but the hospital didn't intend to release her until all the blood tests had been analyzed. Wella waited two hours. When it became clear she had missed the connecting flight and the results still weren't in, she disconnected herself from the monitors and IV and walked out, Tim directing the nurses, in Wella's roiling wake, to bill their insurance. They caught a plane home to California.

"It was full blown after that. Just full-blown panic attacks. A lot of them," Wella says. "I couldn't drive, and I got vertigo, too, which came on a little bit later. Just so much pressure I was feeling, I think. I couldn't believe what was going on with Aaron and how fast this all was happening. On top of it all was pre-menopause, and I toughed it out, was taking nothing and did the night sweats and all that. I was ultra-moody and ultra-nervous."

She started to see a therapist, "which was the best thing in the world for me," she confides. "This whole Aaron thing, signing autographs and what does he eat… He was handling it really, really well, but I'm a little shyer and didn't quite know how to deal with it."

A second doctor put Wella on two typical anti-anxiety medications, which helped ward off the panic attacks. "It's real, these panic attacks," she insists. "Do you know what I would be like without these pills? The panic feels *completely* real for me. I'm still on those medications. To be honest, I don't notice any difference in myself, but Tim thinks I'm not *as* nervous, and there have been no more panic attacks."

She bristles, remembering a recent article deriding anxiety medications, in which a celebrity was calling medication a crutch. Wella defends the legitimate need for those types of medications: "It's not a 'dirty little secret'! People need this stuff to get through the days. It's an affliction, the way you are wired."

Wella pauses to reflect.

So… is this why she runs and swims so obsessively, to help her cope with anxiety?

"*One hundred and fifty percent.*" She punctuates each word of her answer. "I wouldn't have been able to make it without exercise. No way. I don't drink, and I don't do destructive things that other people would do to self-medicate."

A cresting wave of research backs up Wella's theory. A natural reaction to stress, anxiety can shift into high gear, possibly spurred by an imbalance in the chemical messenger serotonin (a neurotransmitter that helps regulate mood), which may manifest in the panic symptoms Wella describes. Several cutting-edge studies are exploring the notion of exercise as a means of treating and possibly preventing anxiety, as well as depression and other mental health issues.[60]

In threatening situations, the human nervous system is primed to react with sweating, dizziness, racing heartbeats—the fight-or-flight response. People sensitive to those symptoms can feel anxious or fearful and may even be predisposed to panic disorders, according to an article citing Jasper Smits, PhD, co-director of the Anxiety Research and Treatment Program at Southern Methodist University in Dallas. Smits and colleague Michael Otto note the similar physical reactions resulting from both exercise and panic attacks, and say their studies suggest that a good exercise regimen could help ward off panic attacks by retraining the brain to more readily accept those symptoms as non-threatening.[61]

Dr. John Ratey, a clinical associate professor of psychiatry at Harvard, shares another perspective on the subject in his book *Spark: The Revolutionary New Science of Exercise and the Brain*. He recounts a spat played out in the *New England Journal of Medicine* in 2004: Cardiologists wrote a letter chastising psychiatrists who were only treating anxiety patients with pharmacologic agents and psychotherapy. The cardiologists who signed the letter highlighted that anxiety puts people at risk for heart problems, and they advocated for more proactive treatment of anxiety through exercise. "Exercise training has been shown to lead to reductions of more than 50 percent in the prevalence of the symptoms of anxiety," the cardiologists wrote. "This supports exercise training as an additional method to reduce chronic anxiety."

Ratey adds that atrial natriuretic peptide, or ANP, a hormone secreted by the heart muscles during exercise, stems the flow of epinephrine in our bodies, lowering the heart rate; and that "seems to reduce the feeling of anxiousness."[62]

Dr. Tracy Greer, of UT Southwestern Medical Center's Mood Disorders Research Program and Clinic in Dallas, has collaborated on several studies in which exercise is prescribed to patients with depression. "We believe that exercising is acting in the brain the same ways as anti-depressants would, in dealing with norepinephrine, dopamine, serotonin, and other neural chemicals," Greer notes.[63]

Research demonstrates that retraining the brain, using systems such as cognitive behavioral therapy, works about as well as the use of selective serotonin reuptake inhibitors (SSRIs)—drugs believed to regulate serotonin, presently used in treating anxiety and depression.[64] Good therapy helps reroute the brain's fear circuitry, the drugs assist the body in regulating serotonin levels, and exercise functions as a means of active coping.

"By activating the sympathetic nervous system through exercise, you break free from the trap of passively waiting and worrying," writes Ratey. "I think combining medicine with exercise can be a great approach. Medicine provides immediate safety, and exercise gets at the fundamentals of anxiety."[65]

* * *

THE LEE AND JOE JAMAIL TEXAS SWIMMING CENTER (TSC) perches on the edge of the gently rolling, Mediterranean-style campus of the University of Texas at Austin, overlooking tiled roofs and limestone architecture. Inside the modern TSC, two long banners suspended from the soaring ceiling boast the famous faces of swimmers who made good under Coach Eddie Reese at this very venue. On the left side, smack in the center, is the highly recognizable smile of Aaron Peirsol, dripping with victory, left hand held high, flashing an extended index and little finger in the Longhorns' traditional "Hook 'Em Horns" sign.

UT's pool is what seasoned swimmers call "fast," engineered to minimize drag and to absorb the waves from swimmers. In it, 1.5 million gallons of water circulate round the clock. The depth of the pool, its gutter system, filtration rate, lane width, and power-operated bulkheads that allow for both short- and long-course events are all calibrated to make this pool a premier racing venue. Considered one of the world's finest competitive swim facilities for aquatic events, it was modeled after the pool built in Munich, Germany, for the 1972 Olympics.[66]

More than the allure of the swim facility, the campus, or the free-spirited city of Austin, it was Coach Edwin Charles "Eddie" Reese that drew Aaron to the program. Serendipitously born on the same day, July 23, though forty-two years apart—Reese in 1941 and Aaron in 1983—the two first met during the 2000 Olympics, when Reese was serving as assistant coach for the US swim team. Reese had distinguished himself as a high-school swimmer (two times a state champion in the tough 200-yard individual medley events) and in collegiate swimming, in the water-centric state of Florida.

He had been head coach of the University of Texas's swimming and diving team since moving from his position as head coach of Auburn in 1978, five years before Aaron was even born. Over his nearly four decades of coaching NCAA teams to titles, Reese has been selected US Olympic men's swim team coach three times, ASCA[67] Coach of the Year three times, and NCAA Coach of the Year eight times, as of this writing. Assistant coach Kris Kubik, who has worked thirty years alongside Reese, was an asset as well, in Aaron's opinion, a seasoned and soft-spoken confidant for the swimmers.

"I just fit in here," Aaron says simply, in hindsight. "For me, it was between [University of California] Berkeley and UT. Something in me was just interested in something very, very different… Something in me was saying to branch out a little bit. I went to a team, where I didn't know many guys, to grow, to have a coach who was very wise in the sport."

"I read about him first," Reese recalls, about recruiting Aaron. "I knew he was world ranked as a fifteen-year-old, which is almost unheard of. He's got a genuine gift, a feel for the water and technique. He has the gift of not slowing down. That goes physically and mentally."

During his career at Texas, Peirsol was honored as 2003 NCAA Swimmer of the Year. He won the 200-meter backstroke event at the National Championships in each of his two seasons before turning professional, and, in only two collegiate seasons, Aaron earned six NCAA championships and eleven All-American certificates.[68]

Trying to define why Aaron was such a standout, Reese ticks off some criteria. "You've gotta have a certain amount of talent. You've gotta work hard. And it takes time. There are some people who swim that, no matter what they do, won't make the Olympics. Obviously Aaron and his sister come from a very talented family," Coach Reese explains, in a gruff Southern drawl, seasoned by years of shouting commands over splashes and echoes.

He also admits, "I was scared to death when he came here. 'Cause he'd already gone so fast." But if the coach had any hesitation about the speedy freshman, it was soon put to rest.

"For someone like Aaron to get better, he must get stronger, train harder and farther. He did all of this. It was easier than I thought," Reese declares.[69] Then, drawing a droll parallel characteristic of his dry sense of humor, Reese describes what it is like to watch Aaron practice: "You know, if you grow up in the Taj Mahal, it's just where you live. It's no big deal. When you see Aaron swim, it's no big deal. But when you see him move out of his lane and move over three to go first in another lane, to race someone in butterfly or freestyle, you know what kind of mentality he's got. He loves to race."[70]

Assistant coach Kubik agrees. "Aaron's greatest gift in sport is that he absolutely hates losing way, way more than he likes winning," he says. "It doesn't matter if it is a swimming race, a pick-up game of basketball, or a running challenge. He also pays astute attention to detail and has constantly sought out ways to improve his strength, his stroke technique, his starts and turns, and his racing strategy. He has learned from his own experiences and continually tweaks what he does to be better each time he races."[71]

Coach Reese reiterates the importance of a hard-driving work ethic that pushes a swimmer to achieve. "Yeah, they're all working hard," he drawls. "But you can always go more. One guy did nine workouts a week in the water, as well as dry land [workouts], weights, three hundred push-ups a night for four months—got him about fifteen hundredths of a second. The C students who had to work to get it are going to do the best here."

Kubik also points out how Aaron's character differs from that of many intense athletes: "Aaron races everything from the start of practice (which is supposed to be a slow, gradual warm-up) all the way until its conclusion. Yet he has a great deal of fun in practice, too. When he is on the wall between sets his mouth is always talking—sometimes he's cracking a joke with other swimmers or with his coaches, sometimes he is encouraging others, sometimes he is offering stroke advice. He rarely is not involved with what those around him are doing. If you watch him for more than about five minutes, you will notice that he is doing something in the water to entertain either himself or everyone else."[72]

Aaron himself views things another way. "I was very talented," he begins, in a manner that does not sound the least bit conceited. "I felt and understood I had a better feel for backstroke than most anyone else. I had great coaches and training partners and a great support system. And I learned the value of hard work as a kid. All those, added up, proved to be potent enough to give me the confidence to believe that I belonged up there. I don't know if it was something that drove me not to lose as much as I saw no reason not to win."[73]

"He is at the top of any good list," recaps Reese. "He is first class. He is very smart and thoughtful. Most of his thoughts are about others. The combination of talent and work ethic has set him apart."

As for the mom behind the swimmer, Reese replies to questions about her with a smile and a well-intentioned jab at Wella's protective nature, a question of his own: "How many times did Wella call to check on Aaron? A lot, but it was and is never a bother. She is a great mom and can call any time."[74]

With the silver from Sydney already under his belt, Aaron continued racking up successes. He set his first world record in 2002, in the 200-meter backstroke. He won three golds, a silver, and a bronze at the 2002 FINA World Swimming Championships in Moscow, where he also broke the world record in the 200-meter backstroke and in the 4x100-meter medley relay. In Yokohama, Japan, at the 2002 Pan Pacific Swimming Championships, he took gold in both the 100- and 200-meter backstroke events and again in the 4x100-meter medley relay, swimming with Brendan Hansen, Michael Phelps, and Jason Lezak, as they set another World Record. Highlights of 2003 included gold in the 100- and 200-meter backstroke events and the 4x100-meter medley relay at the World Aquatics Championships in Barcelona, where Hayley also won a silver medal. And he just continued to shave off the seconds.

By 2004, his sophomore year, Aaron decided to turn pro, giving up his college eligibility to accept a multi-year contract with Nike before the summer Olympics. He was twenty years old. But in a case of "if it ain't broke don't fix it," he continued to train at the TSC under Coaches Reese and Kubik. Amazingly, and to his credit—given the stream of competitions and the endless hours of practice and professional obligations—Aaron graduated with his degree in government in 2006.

Wella is proud he finished. As she points out, "Education is so important to be able to speak with people."

As vital as the work ethic, however, seemed to be the counterbalance of play.

Whenever he could get back to Newport Beach before trials or championships, Aaron still loved to relax by surfing. Across from the Corona del Mar beach, which he and his siblings remember so fondly, is the Balboa Peninsula. On the tip of that spit of land crashes a notorious break, known locally as The Wedge.

"Sometimes, close to Nationals or Olympic Trials, I would get in the car and go check on Aaron," confides Wella, who relates tales of surfer daring and the serious injuries and deaths inflicted by the waves that periodically rise to thirty feet and barrel over a relatively shallow stretch of shore there.

While most athletes would be forbidden by coaches or their own caution to risk injuring themselves prior to competition, Aaron's way of escaping the stress was to return to his first love, the ocean. A popular YouTube video

TOP: *Wella stood among these gnarled trees to watch Aaron bodysurf The Wedge.*
CENTER LEFT: *Gentle waves roll onto Newport Beach.*
CENTER RIGHT: *The path runs along Newport Beach.*
BOTTOM: *Houses face the ocean along Newport Beach.*
PHOTOS: LAURA COTTAM SAJBEL

shows Aaron bodysurfing The Wedge, his style the proverbial poetry in motion.[75] Wella, concerned yet understanding her son's need to unwind, would hike from the road to the scraggly stand of gnarled, wind-twisted trees overlooking the beach and watch Aaron from a distance.[76]

North along that same beach is 11th Street, where Aaron and his friends hung out in high school and learned to surf. The wide, flat stretch of sand that is Newport Beach runs miles, through Huntington and on up to Seal Beach. All along, the beach is bordered on the east by a broad concrete pathway, frequented by runners and skateboarders passing right in front of homes with an ocean view. It's easy to understand the appeal this place holds for Aaron: Here, he is just another one of the guys gleefully bodysurfing in the ocean.

* * *

THERE'S A BANNER AT THE JAMES E. MARTIN AQUATICS CENTER on the Auburn campus, too. Hayley thinks it's funny that her likeness looms larger than that of César Cielo, another Auburn alum, who won gold in the 50-meter freestyle at the Beijing Olympics and holds world records in the 50- and 100-meter freestyle events.

In college, at Auburn, Hayley was part of a winning team that earned three women's NCAA championship titles and four Southeastern Conference (SEC) titles. She also earned two individual NCAA titles, as well as three individual SEC titles, in the 1,650-yard freestyle during her junior and senior years at Auburn. At the Pan Pacific Championships in August 2006, Hayley became the third woman in history to break sixteen minutes in the 1,500-meter freestyle, behind only Janet Evans and Kate Ziegler.

But Hayley had already proven her skills by her junior and senior years in high school.

"Hayley really made her mark in 2002, when she qualified for Pan Pacs and the 2003 World Championships in Europe," Nova coach Brent Lorenzen notes. Pan Pacific Championships was her first big qualifying swim, but Lorenzen had fully expected her to make it.

Hayley broke down in tears when she found out she had qualified and would be flying to Japan to compete. She could still feel a little shy, and the prospect of such a distant, international meet was daunting. Luckily, Tim and Wella realized Michael Phelps, a promising swimmer near Hayley's age, would be going, too. They asked him to look after Hayley, and they called

Aaron in to assuage her concerns. The anecdote underscores how young these elite athletes are and how quickly they have to grow up, traveling on their own, away from family, on trans-oceanic flights to competitions.

Hayley was ranked seventh in the world in 800-meter freestyle by her senior year of high school,[77] so colleges around the country actively recruited her. As Wella recalls, the family had finished up the rounds of looking at colleges and swim programs: USC, Auburn, Florida, Arizona, University of Georgia. Wella had been particularly struck by Jack Bauerle at Georgia and his assistant, Harvey Humphries. She and Tim really thought Hayley was leaning that way, too. However, Auburn assistant coaches Ralph Crocker and Kim Brackin knocked on their door and changed all that.

"It's a cute story," Wella reveals. The family had previously met with Auburn head coach Dave Marsh, but Ralph, the distance coach—endurance being Hayley's strong suit—won everyone over in his visit to their home with his warmth and personality. After the door closed behind Ralph and Kim, Hayley announced, "I really like him." Wella chuckles.

"You'd think the kids would sit down and talk about this. You know, Aaron just came downstairs and announced [two years before] that he was going to Texas!" she exclaims. After the meeting with Ralph, "Hayley just ran up the stairs and said, 'I'm going to Auburn!'"

Wella and Tim had never been to Auburn.

Luckily, it was a good choice for Hayley. Around Auburn, intimates Wella with a smile, "there was nothing going on." Wella worried that Hayley, whom Aaron has fondly called "the life of the party," would be distracted from swimming if there were too many entertaining activities on campus or in town. Given Hayley's boundless energy, Wella often comments, "Thank God we had the pool for Hayley," insinuating that—as with her own teenage self—an unfocused Hayley could have gotten into trouble.

"My mom's funny," Hayley retorts now. "I like to have fun and go out. I think she was *so* overprotective.

"I went to Auburn, in Alabama, subconsciously, to get completely out of the bubble of Newport Beach. If you can take yourself out of these places, you get an objective viewpoint. Newport Beach was all about materialism and wealth."

She majored in criminology. "I am fascinated by criminal minds," she says. "What choices and decisions they make. We could all potentially be that person!" Really, though, her focus was on her teammates and their sport. Looking back, she comments that as an athlete with a scholarship, she managed to skip some necessary life skills: "Everything was done for you. I never paid rent. Never booked a flight until I was twenty-three years old."

For building a close-knit social group, however, the situation was ideal. As a team, she believes the swimmers were so good because they were so close: "We were all on the same page, saw each other every day. We didn't want to do anything to impede our goal of National Champions.

"I loved Auburn—the people, the small college town, how everyone was so into the school. At college," Hayley explains, "it was competing for the team. We were all working toward one goal, and I liked the camaraderie."

Again, elite swimming is a tight circle. Ralph Crocker had been coached himself by Eddie Reese. And later, after coaching at Auburn, Kim Brackin spent some time as the women's swim coach at the University of Texas, with Eddie.

Crocker worked with all the swimmers, but primarily he presided over the distance group, or, as his swimmers affectionately nicknamed it, Ralph's House of Pain (RHOP), for his challenging workouts. Their pool was rated, in the 2002 issue of *Sports Illustrated*, as the third fastest in the country, according to the university's sports website, but that wasn't all that contributed to their success.

The swimmers adored Ralph, Hayley says: "Ralph was just one of the sweetest men I have ever met, a gentle soul. We could trust him so much. He was everything good. His wife, Margaret, is the same—a good, good person. He took me in like his little daughter. I was by far the closest to him on the team." Ralph's emphasis was on creating good human beings with character and holding his swimmers accountable for their actions. "He was the person I learned the most from, being away at school."

"Hayley loved Ralph like a second father," Wella says. "She saw the good in Ralph. She'd go out to lunch with him and her friends. And he stayed at the hospital with Hayley when she was so sick at World Trials."

Hayley's experience at the 2003 World Trials, a qualifying meet for the FINA[78] World Championships, illustrates both Ralph's and Hayley's dedication. Hayley, then a freshman, ran a high fever with some sort of stomach virus and was hospitalized overnight on an IV, the evening before her 800-meter race. Her coach stayed at the foot of her bed throughout the ordeal.

Former YMCA coach Stacey Zapolski had the chance to watch Hayley and Aaron compete at that particular World Trial event: "Hayley had spent the night before in a hospital after becoming very sick. The next day she still swam in the eight hundred free, which is a testimony to her personal strength. She held on for as long as she could but ultimately finished third in the event." Only the top two finishers go on to World Championships.

Zapolski had been on the phone with Wella, who could not attend the meet. "Wella was crying for her daughter, yet Hayley was so composed," Zapolski recalls. "My guess is Hayley knew she did the best she could, considering the circumstances, but I am sure she was greatly disappointed."

Shortly after Hayley's race, Aaron won the 100-meter backstroke event. "I literally cried as I watched her go over to him and hug him," Zapolski says. Hayley could justifiably have wallowed in self-pity, yet she was truly happy for her brother's success.

"In many ways, Hayley has lived her athletic career in Aaron's shadow, as his Olympic success has brought him much more attention. The amazing thing about her, though, is this has never bothered her," comments Zapolski. "She has always been her brother's biggest supporter, as she, more than anyone, can relate to what he is experiencing.

"I have to believe that Wella, as a mom, helped create this environment since they were very young. Somehow Wella succeeded in raising her kids to really love each other, and that was probably the most amazing thing she

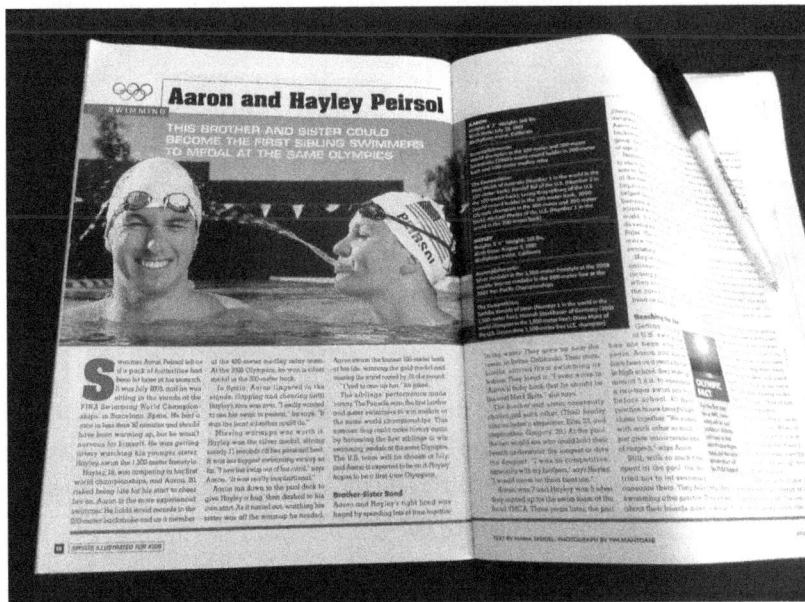

Articles about the siblings appeared in newspapers and magazines, like this Sports Illustrated for Kids, speculating that both of them might make the Olympics and highlighting their close relationship. PHOTO COURTESY OF WELLA HARTIG

could do."

Despite the initial loss, Hayley aced her second race at World Trials, so that both she and Aaron qualified to swim in Barcelona, Spain, at the 2003 FINA World Championships. Hayley won a silver medal there in the 1,500-meter freestyle, while Aaron took gold in the 100- and 200-meter backstroke events and in the 4x100-meter medley relay. They are, so far, the only sibling duo to medal at these championships.

One of the things Aaron believes cemented the bond between him and Hayley was the time they spent together at meets. "Our parents couldn't always go, but it was so important for both of us to be there for each other," he remarks. Sharing so many of the same pressures, experiences, and achievements gave Aaron and Hayley a deep reverence for each other's strengths. "That silver medal [in Barcelona] was one of the coolest things to watch," Aaron remembers. "I swam fifteen minutes later but watched her race, watched when I should have been warming up. I don't remember a thing about my race but everything about hers."

When Ralph Crocker got sick, his swimmers thought he would beat the cancer. He went into remission, but then the disease came back with a vengeance.

"I saw him in hospice," Hayley recalls quietly. "He was just a shell, but his spirit was there. He needed to go; it was the end. When you lose someone, it's so, so sad, but it is life. I tried to do things in honor of him, live as if he were still there."

She admits that Crocker's death in January 2007, her senior year of college, may have spurred her on to faster times. "I'll carry that for the rest of my life," she says. "I am so glad I had him in my life for five or six years." Hayley was climbing into the elite ranks, earning individual titles at NCAA and international events. In 2006, she finished the 1,500-meter freestyle in 15:57.36, the third woman in the world to do so under sixteen minutes. During the summers of 2006 and 2007, Hayley trained for Nationals with Club Wolverine in Ann Arbor, Michigan, under Bob Bowman and "legendary distance guru" Jon Urbanchek.

One Sunday around 4:30 a.m., Hayley awoke to the light in the hall. Her roommate was there but could not possibly be up yet. "Justine could sleep through a bomb. We had to wake her up every day for practice," Hayley begins. But then, peeking out from the blanket, she saw a large man silhouetted in the doorway. She tried to rationalize the situation, thinking for a moment it might be a friend. *Oh my God*, she suddenly realized, *he's standing between my room and Justine's; something is terribly wrong.*

"He came into my room, and I hopped out of bed. He lunged at me to cover my face," she remembers. "I have never screamed like that before—guttural, for survival," Luckily, he turned and ran. As he was running out, Justine woke up. They discovered the intruder had broken in through a screen on the balcony. "He had had to scale the building and climb a pole to our balcony. We had locked ourselves out before and knew how hard it was to get in," Hayley says.

Not thinking clearly, the girls tried to call Bob Bowman and a few other people, none of whom answered at that hour. Finally, they reached their friend Andrew, who picked them up and took them to his house. "Even when he came," Hayley recalls, "I was still screaming." Nonetheless, Hayley and Justine went on to practice that morning, just a few hours later. When they returned to their apartment afterward, the sliding door was wide open, so they finally called police. The intruder had returned. He had taken a computer and rummaged but obviously hadn't come to rob them.

"The police said we had to move out, that we were dealing with someone willing to come back—willing to risk to get what he wanted," Hayley concludes. "He knew the layout of the apartment, and we had such a strict schedule—a two-hour practice in the morning, two hours in the afternoon. He had been watching. We were so focused on swimming… What naiveté."

Though Hayley tried to be brave about what had happened, the incident gnawed at her psyche. She later admitted to a *Daily Pilot* reporter than she dealt with post-traumatic stress disorder after the break-in, which eventually turned out to involve someone who had been stalking Hayley and her roommates.[79] That event may have set the stage: Hayley began to waver in the drive that kept her logging distance in the pool for the ten or eleven practices a week that her distance events required.

She went on to defend her 2006 NCAA title in the 1,650-yard freestyle during the NCAA Women's Swimming and Diving Championships in the spring of 2007. Her time (15:45.92) was ten seconds faster than her seeded time, nearly four seconds faster than her previous win, and she set the University of Minnesota pool record.[80] Not long afterward, she would swim in Melbourne, Australia, at the World Championships.

But she had begun taking "copious amounts of Ambien [a short-term sedative for insomnia] and brushed the whole intruder incident under the rug," Hayley relates. "I was fine—only until things started unraveling after Nationals."

She began seeing a therapist but claims she was in denial: "I started partying, smoking—things uncharacteristic of myself. I couldn't run by myself for years, and was very untrusting, especially of men."

"I believe that you have to tread lightly when if comes to sports, because if even the slightest seed of doubt in yourself is planted, you have to be so attentive to it... be careful not to let it grow," Hayley once commented, in talking about competition. "Oftentimes that happens to the best... that doubt in yourself, in your performance, in life. When that happens, it's a scary thing because nothing good can come of doubt."

Those words took on renewed significance in light of her shocking encounter with the intruder.

Within the year, she would walk away from swimming. She contacted former coach Brent Lorenzen and asked to train under him for triathlon. In hindsight, she views the break-in philosophically: "If it hadn't happened, I may have gone in a different direction. Maybe I wouldn't have found my way, myself. I went into a bit of a spiral, and people were concerned. Then I decided to do multi-sport [triathlon]. I was probably running away, wanting to distract myself. There was anger, because how could he affect my life so much? I mean, *How dare you?*

"I was this young girl, and I had these goals. When he came into my room, I did not look into the eyes of what could have been my demise."

Chapter 11 : Respect

Wella's Tip for Staying Afloat: *Aaron kept a poster up in his room that read, "Only with adversity comes greatness."*

AT NATIONALS, HELD IN MINNEAPOLIS IN 2002, AARON had topped even his Olympic highlight by breaking the world record set by Lenny Krayzelburg in 1999.[81]

"The first time he broke a world record, we weren't there," Wella says. Tim was watching on the computer at work, narrating the race to her over the phone. She was standing in the kitchen, just home from work. "The racers looked like ponies, the way they used to show events from above the pool. Tim was saying, 'He's just off the third wall, ahead of world record pace... Wella, he broke the world record!'"

When Aaron returned from that race, cheerleaders from Newport Beach High School were at the airport to greet him, along with friends and family and other admirers. Among the crowd was Dan Albano, a sports reporter who had been following and writing about Aaron's rocketing career; he brought along his wife and baby for the momentous occasion.

"We're not from a small town," Wella points out, "but when someone does something as extraordinary as Aaron was doing, it became a smaller community and people pulled together."

Aaron's work ethic and talent had taken the family places Wella had never even imagined. But as the competition grew relentlessly tougher, it was hard for her to watch. The Olympics at Sydney had been "a really enchanting time," she remembers, looking back after countless other pressure-cooker events. "I was just a baby, so innocent of what this sport is. You really have to learn it on your own. No one ever said to me, 'I know what you're going through.' I would have gobbled that up." She remembers fretting after every conversation with Aaron, whether he sounded relaxed or tired or stressed, and absorbing the pressure of each race herself.

"I wasn't so anxious when I was younger; I just wasn't prepared for the success of the kids," she muses.

Former Y coach Stacey Zapolski, who still coaches age-group swimmers, has remained friends with the family and has followed many of Aaron's and Hayley's races.

"It is natural for the rest of the swimming world to want to knock him off that top spot, and for most swimmers, that would be unbearable pressure year after year," Zapolski comments. "Yet, somehow, Aaron has dealt with this pressure with such dignity and grace. I think Wella has shown her children that there are so many wonderful things for them outside the pool. He is far from being self-absorbed when he can ask about *my* children seconds before getting in and swimming the prelims at Worlds!"

"Some people can't succeed under the pressure at the Olympic level," Wella says. "It is *indescribable* pressure. You only have that chance every four years. A lot of really good people are still on the sidelines—they still have those dreams. It's *so* tough to make it to the top.

"The parents have to be a really big part of it—you can't be a downer. Express no negativity or advice. Keep your mouth shut so the swimmers can listen to their coaches."

By 2004, Aaron was king of the 100- and 200-meter backstroke events, which he'd won at World Championships, and he was favored to win both events heading into Olympic Trials preceding the Olympic Games in Athens that summer. A sophomore at UT by then, Aaron called Tim one morning in January to share some distressing news. Tim notes that Aaron and Hayley often called him first if they had a problem. "I think they thought I was a softer landing place for those times," Tim intimates, being that the kids tried to forestall Wella's fretting.

Aaron and Hayley had grown to love and respect that about Tim. "Wella's initial overreaction may be something they couldn't deal with," he explains, "though Wella and I come around to the same reaction eventually. Bottom line: She loves those kids so much. She literally would go to the ends of the earth. But there are times we have to tell her to back off. To her credit, she has listened and respected that."

Aaron, in training for the NCAA championships slated for March as well as for the Olympic Trials later that spring, was set to defend the 200-meter backstroke title he had won as a freshman, when he had set an American record. However, he reported to Tim that bright January day in 2004 that he thought he had mononucleosis and was awaiting the results of a blood test that would give a definitive diagnosis.

"Our heads were spinning as we pondered the ramifications of the news and how it could affect Aaron's dreams and goals. We found out a couple of days later that he indeed had the disease, but it was considered a mild case," Tim says. The plan was for Coach Reese to back off Aaron's training a bit, but there didn't have to be any interruption on the whole. Although still weakened by the effects of the illness, Aaron did successfully defend his 200-meter backstroke title at NCAAs.

Now the focus narrowed to Olympic Trials, to be held in Long Beach, California. At stake was a second Olympics, a chance for Aaron to sign endorsement contracts and turn professional, giving up the eligibility to swim his last two years in college. Tim and Wella, hoping to allow Aaron to concentrate on his workouts, interviewed agents who wanted to represent him. At the time, there were only two agencies that represented swimmers at all. Evan Morgenstein of PMG (Premier Management Group) Sports had recently added to his staff former Olympic backstroker Bobby Brewer, whom Aaron knew.[82] Aaron seemed comfortable with Morgenstein, and Tim realized Morgenstein was one of the first sports agents to successfully negotiate deals for athletes who weren't yet world famous.

"Because of Aaron's age and the fact we didn't want him thinking about anything but swimming, I would work with Evan as a sounding board for the offers that would come in," recalls Tim. Before long, Morgenstein had negotiated a plum contract with Nike that would run from 2004 through 2008. Aaron could concentrate fully on the upcoming Olympic Trials.

Meanwhile Hayley, too, was gearing up for the Olympic Trials. She had begun her freshman year at Auburn, then returned to California to train under her former club coach, Brent Lorenzen, for her specialty: the 800-meter freestyle event. Luckily the trials were near home, so Wella, Tim, Aaron, and Hayley could sleep at the house and maintain some semblance of a normal life.

According to Wella, Lorenzen hadn't wanted Hayley to go away for college before the Olympic Trials. He had concerns about the vagaries of a freshman in a new environment.

"It was a bad year, considering there were college parties, tempting to a freshman," Wella recalls of the transition. But Hayley had been determined to start at Auburn. She returned from college with a slightly changed stroke and a few added pounds. At the level where hundredths of a second can count, those changes may have made the difference.

Tim says, "Hayley finished fifth in the 800-meter free. We were proud of her making an Olympic Trial final, which is a huge accomplishment in itself. Most people would be happy for a lifetime to have done what she did."

The Olympic Trials went absolutely according to plan for Aaron. He won both the 100-meter and 200-meter backstroke events (beating a pretty good swimmer named Michael Phelps, who had decided he wanted to swim the 200-meter backstroke). Aaron also broke his own world record in the 200-meter backstroke.

* * *

ONCE AARON WAS ON THE TEAM, Wella and Tim made their travel arrangements. The Nike contract adjusted Aaron's compensation to allow his parents to travel with him. To further assist, Wella's brother-in-law, Henry, had patients whose family in Athens invited Wella and Tim to stay at their home.

When they arrived that summer for the Olympics, Wella and Tim settled into the downstairs flat of an older Greek couple, who quickly made them feel welcome.

"It ended up being the experience of a lifetime, as the neighborhood and surrounding areas were authentic Greek culture," Tim says. "The first night we had fresh tomatoes and feta cheese with fresh bread out on their upstairs patio. Later the husband played guitar and sang songs." Of course, the Greek couple spoke little if any English, and Wella and Tim spoke no Greek at all. "But," Tim points out, "it is amazing how you can communicate on a certain level."

Their hosts also arranged for a driver named Tasos, whom Wella and Tim could call at any hour to taxi them around Athens.

Nike had taken over a small private college as the site for hosting the athletes sponsored by the company. Wella and Tim were delighted to find that gave them full access to a beautiful 25-meter outdoor pool and the campus gym, where they took advantage of the treadmills in lieu of running in the heat of the city. They had fun people-watching at the center, as the famous athletes sponsored by Nike, including the US basketball team, traipsed through to avail themselves of comfortable seating, televisions, computers, and fabulous fruits, pastas, and desserts. One of the perks was a coffee bar that would concoct Wella's favorite iced coffee each day.

International meets, including the Olympics, hold the 100-meter back-stroke event prior to the 200-meter event. So Aaron's first event gave him a chance to settle into the venue. He breezed through the prelims and semi-finals and was set to swim the final as the favorite, the following night.

The Athens pool was an outdoor facility, a rarity for the Olympic games. The night of the 100-meter backstroke final, the wind was blowing 30 miles an hour and affected the backstrokers, as the arms go higher in the air than they do in other strokes. It had been thought that Aaron might break the world record in the final, but the wind was blowing the swimmers off course. Aaron managed to win his first gold medal in that event, and Wella and Tim were ecstatic. To celebrate, they invited Wella's sister Patte and her husband, Henry, to a local restaurant suggested by Tasos. "We invited Tasos to go get his wife and have dinner with us, too," Tim says.

Aaron's second race, the 200-meter backstroke event, was scheduled for a few days later, so Wella and Tim settled into a routine of running and swimming at the Nike center before setting out for some sight-seeing each day. "Our favorite was going to the Parthenon and seeing how amazing Greek culture was, to have built this magnificent structure with no modern means. The view took in all of Athens and really was awe-inspiring," Tim remembers. Tim and Wella had finally, officially, gotten married in April, and the trip to Athens provided a bit of a honeymoon.

Tim and Wella loved visiting the Parthenon, overlooking Athens. PHOTO COURTESY OF WELLA HARTIG

The 200-meter backstroke preliminaries and semi-finals went smoothly, and Aaron was seeded first, heading into the next evening's final. His times were a second or so faster than the next competitor, and the family felt confident Aaron would win. Wella got her hair styled by Tasos's wife in what she called the "Beverly Hills" section of Athens, where there were gorgeous parks and restaurants.

She and Tim arrived early at the swim complex, feeling happy that there was no wind and that the conditions were good. Aaron swam a beautiful race, winning by almost two full seconds, with an Olympic-record time of 1:54.95. Tim and Wella hugged and jumped up and down—until suddenly the scoreboard flashed "DSQ," indicating disqualification, next to Aaron's name.

Exactly what happened that day depends on which of the flurry of articles and reports one reads. The San Francisco Chronicle best described the atmosphere in an aptly titled article, "Pool of Utter Mix-Ups: Peirsol at First DQ'd, Then Given the Gold." Writes Mark Fainaru-Wada:

> **2004-08-20 04:00:00 PST Athens** — Thursday night at the pool featured a disqualification, then a reversal of the disqualification, then protests of the reversal of the disqualification. Not to mention some nationalistic innuendo, a judge with a language barrier he couldn't overcome, an unintelligible statement by swimming's world governing body, a weeping mother who managed to break down the Olympics' ubiquitous security force and, finally, an announcement that the next day there would be an explanation of a previous explanation.
>
> You just can't make this stuff up.[83]

Aaron touched first, with an Olympic record of 1:54.95. Markus Rogan took second with a time of 1:57.35, followed by Razvan Florea in 1:57.56. Though accounts differ and rumors abound (since Aaron had earlier accused a breaststroker of winning gold with an illegal kick), the fallout seems to be that the French judge took issue with Aaron's turn and pull at the third wall of the race. The race was reviewed and Aaron's gold medal restored, but the pandemonium that ensued spoiled the excitement of the win. Wella, worked into a protective-mother fervor, muscled herself and Tim past the wall of security to the pool deck, but then she was overcome with emotion and had to be tended by US officials and team doctors. Moments later, the disqualification was overturned, and Aaron was awarded the gold.

"But it took the moment away from Wella and me," explains Tim. "We both still get tears in our eyes these years later, recounting the pain of that moment and how we never will get back that special moment we should have had."

While Wella contends that the controversy was politically motivated and was devastated that the judge stole the glory of the win from Aaron, she admits that the incident also brought out the good in some people, too.

In the midst of the confusion and upset, the mother of Australian swimmer Matt Welsh (whose record Aaron had bested in Moscow) found Wella.

"She was *wonderful*," Wella remembers. "She came over to me and said, 'I'm Matt Welsh's mom,' and I just put my head down on her. It took a lot for her to come down the stairs and find me," Wella emphasizes, referring to the byzantine security measures that corral the spectators from the athletes. The way another mother reached out really touched Wella, who has never forgotten the kindness.

Markus Rogan, a Stanford swimmer originally from Austria, won silver and would have benefited most from Aaron's disqualification. Rogan, accepting his medal on behalf of Austria—the country's first Olympic swimming medal since 1912—told reporters, "It is an historic moment for my country. But there are many more important events in this world than an Olympic medal. This is an Olympic moment, to share the podium with someone from another continent who is also my best friend."[84]

Aaron—ever positive—recalls that event in an entirely different light from Wella and Tim.

"That is my favorite moment in my swimming career," he counters, his voice rising with enthusiasm. "If that wouldn't have happened, there are certain things about myself that would have slipped by. The gold medal didn't mean anything, at the end of the day," he recognizes. "I was walking back toward the warm-up pool, doing some deep thinking. Why was I not throwing chairs, not despondent? I knew I didn't do anything wrong, but I realized that I was going to be able to walk away and be fine.

"I was so happy. The gold medal was a thing to focus on, in a broad sense, but it was all the little things in the process. Holy cow, I was able to touch *first* in an *Olympic race.* That moment I learned why I did what I did. I learned why I put in all that work," he reflects.

"It was because I was allowed to do something I really loved. That was the biggest gift my mom gave me.

"Medals sit in drawers," he philosophizes. "They are symbols of something much more important. What mom gave us, in that way, is that she was able to overcome [her circumstances]. It's not about the medals. It's about us being good kids and being happy. Being good people."

In an example of Wella's teaching coming back to hold her to task, Aaron quietly suggests, "I have control over my own feelings. I can choose whether to freak out or not. And I know what was important. It took that [mix-up in Athens] for me to learn. [Stuff] like that happens and you deal with it."

Aaron's final event was the 4x100-meter medley relay, which the American team won. Because he swims the lead-off leg of the race, Aaron's time counted officially, and he broke the world record in the 100-meter backstroke again during that race.

During the ceremonies, in which the Greek hosts placed olive wreaths on the heads of the winning athletes as a nod to the ancient Olympic tradition,[85] no one looked more fitting in that headwear than golden-haired Aaron Peirsol, the modern Greek god.

Back home in Orange County, Aaron's gold medals made the front page. COURTESY OF WELLA HARTIG

Chapter 12 : Triumph

Wella's Tip for Staying Afloat: *Be there to share the moment. In Aaron, there's something like electricity in his eyes you don't want to miss. And you shouldn't have to miss that.*

THE SUCCESS KEPT ROLLING IN A BLUR OF WORLD CHAMPIONSHIPS, Pan Pacific Championships, and World Aquatics Championships. In 2006, Hayley and Aaron made a splash at Nationals, being siblings who both captured titles. Hayley, still at Auburn but representing Club Wolverine, where she had been training during the summers in Michigan under Jon Urbanchek, turned in the second-fastest time in the world for that event that year (8:26.45), beating world champion Kate Ziegler in the 800-meter freestyle.[86]

Aaron's and Hayley's comments after that meet illustrated the strong sibling relationship the two of them had grown to enjoy. When Hayley won, Aaron declared happily, "My night was done, to tell you the truth. My sister took a lot of pressure off me. Just her doing so well is inspiring in many ways. I already felt like I'd won, even though I hadn't even swum yet." Hayley good-naturedly complained, "I told him I was nervous and he said, 'I bet.' I told him, 'That's not something you say to someone who tells you they are nervous.'"[87]

In other coverage of the same meet, reporter Eli Saslow of the *Washington Post* wrote, "Hayley Peirsol took her turn suffering Wednesday night. She and her brother, Aaron, agree it is much more agonizing to watch each other race than it is to compete.... By the time Aaron finally touched the wall in first place, Hayley looked more exhausted than he did."[88]

As Aaron observes, "It's more powerful to watch the other. We found something more valuable" in each other's support than in individual success. "If we fail, we can brush ourselves off, but watching someone you care for fail is harder."

In 2006, Aaron held nine of the fastest times on earth in the 200-meter

PEIRSOLS
Continued from A10

topping Kate Ziegler, the 2005 world champion in the event, who was second in 8:32.72.

Hayley Peirsol was third after the first 100 and second nearly all of the next 350 meters, before taking the lead at the 500 mark. She led by .23 seconds after 600, then made a move to widen the lead with 150 meters remaining.

"I was like 'It's now or never,'" Hayley Peirsol said of her successful attempt to decrease the chances of Ziegler chasing her down. "[Ziegler, who outdueled Peirsol to win the 400 free earlier in the meet, with Peirsol taking third] is a tough cookie," Hayley Peirsol said. "I was thinking, if I die, I die. But it was fun. That's what I live for is racing."

Haley Peirsol said losing to Ziegler in the 400 free motivated her for the 800.

"That fired me up," said Hayley Peirsol, who spoke with her brother earlier Saturday, hoping

MARK DUSTIN / DAILY PILOT

Hayley Peirsol, left, reaches over to hug Kate Ziegler, right, after Peirsol beat her in the women's 800-meter freestyle Saturday.

he could settle her nerves..

"I told him I was nervous and he said 'I bet you are,'" she said. "I told him, 'That's not something you say to someone who tells you they are nervous.'"

Aaron Peirsol said he was only kidding with his sister and that he always has her best interests at heart.

"I'm very happy for my sister," Aaron Peirsol said. "I wanted her to make the team [the squad representing the USA at the Pan

Pacific Championships, Aug. 17-21 in Victoria, British Columbia, Canada] and she did."

Aaron Peirsol said when Hayley performs well, it usually relaxes him.

"The last time it was like this was when she won a silver at the 2003 world championships," Aaron Peirsol said. "It really inspired me and I won the 100 back that night. It probably won't happen every meet, but it's cool for it to happen once in a while."

Hayley beat reigning champion Kate Ziegler.
COURTESY OF WELLA HARTIG

backstroke event. In 2007, he became the first man to finish the 100-meter backstroke under fifty-three seconds, and held five of the fastest times ever posted in that event as well. But US teammate Ryan Lochte overtook him in the final stretch of the 200-meter event at the World Aquatics Championships in Melbourne to dish out Aaron's first international loss since his silver in Sydney in 2000, seven years earlier.

"It was heartbreaking for us as parents, as well as tough for Aaron to take, as he had been quoted in the past that the two hundred was his 'baby,'" Tim recalls. But Aaron, ever gracious, reached right over the lane line to shake Lochte's hand.

The 2008 Olympic Trials in Omaha, Nebraska, showed off the city's nicely redone downtown. As had become their custom, Wella and Tim found a YMCA with a pool to continue their daily workout, and they ran along the river that runs through Omaha. Tim, reared in Iowa, enjoyed being back in a place with "a Midwest attitude," and they even got good seats for the event, surrounded by other ardent swim fans.

"Throughout his career Aaron has always been able to know just how fast to swim in the preliminaries and semi-finals to get a nice lane in finals. So it was no big surprise to us that Aaron didn't qualify first in each of the prelims and semi-finals for the one hundred [meter backstroke]. But to the people sitting behind us it became a running discussion that maybe Peirsol didn't have what it took anymore," Tim relates.

Fortunately, Aaron proved his mettle, ending up on top, safely on the 2008 Olympic team. A few days later, Aaron again comfortably swam the prelims and semi-finals and qualified first for the next night's final in the 200-meter backstroke. "He swam a beautiful race and won the event, and in the process beat Ryan Lochte to settle the score from World Championships in 2007," Tim concludes.

Again, plans had to be made to travel to the Olympics, to be held in Beijing.

"For once, we knew no one there—strange in a land of billions—and wouldn't be staying in a local neighborhood. We would have to book a normal trip and stay in a hotel," says Tim.

Aaron's girlfriend at the time, Mandy, traveled with them, and Wella and Tim both appreciated her presence. She was good-natured and willing to hang out "with a couple of old people like us," Tim says with a smile.

Unlike the earlier, magical Olympic experiences in Sydney and Athens, Beijing left Wella and Tim cold in many regards. For the first time in nineteen years, they missed more than a day in a row of their treasured swim, unable to find access to a public pool.

"We did find a beautiful park in the midst of where we were staying and were able to run every day there. It would be seven o'clock in the morning, and hundreds, if not thousands, of locals were doing everything from ballroom dancing to badminton, tennis, walking the dogs, stretching, and more. It was very amusing for us, and I actually made friends with some of the runners, who told me in broken English where to show up the next day to run with them, as I decided to leave Wella and Mandy in the dust," Tim teases.

Besides the disappointment of not being able to swim, Wella was disturbed to learn that a poor neighborhood had been demolished to make way for the showy Olympic venues. In addition, it took an hour each way on public transportation for them to get to the Olympic events. Then, the network decided to show the events live to increase ratings and rearranged the swim finals for early morning in Beijing, which Wella and Tim worried would throw Aaron off his game.

"But since swimming is the most popular sport for Olympic coverage— revenue, in corporate speak—the powers that be decided that swimmers would be the ones to make the sacrifice, as everything they've trained for their whole lives pointed toward swimming finals at night," protests Tim. "No other sport had to make this kind of change for these Olympics." From friends, they later heard that the networks back in the States tape-delayed the Olympics, anyway.

Aaron, always looking on the sunny side, wasn't nearly as bothered. "The Water Cube [a nickname for the Beijing National Aquatics Center] was one of those venues in our career where we knew we could only be at an Olympic Games. It was the venue and the architecture, yes, but the atmosphere around it was also quite electrifying, and the smell of the Games was in the air from the day we got there," he says.

"I have competed in other pools that meant more to me, most of them outside and in the elements, but that was, without a doubt, an Olympic venue, with all the bells and whistles of the cheering fans, the lighted walls, amazing pool, and world leaders cheering you on—a surreal experience."

* * *

IN AUGUST OF 2008, THE WATER CUBE IN BEIJING bewitched the world. Fabricated with 22,000 beams of honeycombed steel and 100,000 square feet of clear plastic pneumatic cushioning, the Beijing National Aquatics Center is essentially a bubble-wrapped rectangle that appears to be a cube of burbling water. At night, subtly changing blue and purple lights glow from the building, enhancing the watery illusion from the perspective of the plaza. Inside, the vast facility prompted Aaron to comment to a teammate, "Is it hazy in here?" Indeed, the venue seemed to have its own atmosphere. Not only was the light and ethereal architecture stunning the crowds, but swimmer Michael Phelps had declared his bid to break Mark Spitz's 1972 record of seven gold medals in a single Olympics. While Phelps garnered the press, he was not alone in pulling down all the gold that Americans would take home that year.

In the 100-meter backstroke, Aaron qualified for the final in fifth place, earning an outside lane, rather than the preferred Lane 4. Like the fans at the Trials in Omaha, the media now speculated what might be wrong with the "King of the Backstroke."

"We went to finals that morning wondering if, indeed, he wasn't feeling a hundred percent or what might be going on, as he had never qualified that far down in a world event," Tim says. But their fears quickly dissipated as he dominated the race, capturing in world-record time his second straight gold medal in this event in the Olympic Games. "We had a great time on the subway home, packed in with a zillion Chinese who thought our look and ways were quite interesting," notes Tim.

Wella and Tim were excited now about the 200-meter event, feeling that Aaron was in great shape to win another gold medal. Heading into the final, Aaron had the fastest time. Nike got good seats for the family, but Ryan Lochte edged out Aaron again and took the gold. While they were not shocked, given the 2007 dual in Melbourne, Mandy buried her head in Tim's shoulder and cried for Aaron.

"For once, Wella and I weren't in tears, as we wanted to make sure Mandy felt better, and it actually made the moment easier to deal with, having to think of someone else's feelings rather than concentrating on our own," he admits.

Wella clearly remembers that race, and the effort she and Tim made to find and congratulate Lochte's parents. They feel it is important to be gracious, whether you win or not.

"People need to do more of that," she observes. "It is an amazing feat to beat Aaron Peirsol. It is an amazing feat to get a gold medal."

Arguably one of the most nerve-wracking events of the Games was the men's 4x100-meter medley relay: If the team won, Michael Phelps would have his unprecedented eighth gold medal. Aaron, breaststroker Brendan Hansen, Phelps on the butterfly leg, and freestyler Jason Lezak were pitted against the mighty Australian team and the powerful Japanese. The race was a nail-biter that brought spectators at the Beijing National Aquatics Center to their feet.

With the huge honeycomb of bubbles as backdrop, the swimmers took their places. Peirsol leapt in with the other backstrokers and was last to surface and settle into position at the wall, one of his trademark moves that unnerves competitors.

Aaron swam the first leg of the relay, and the US team won gold in world-record time, landing Phelps his historic eighth gold of the Games.

Aaron's haul from three Olympics was now five gold and two silver medals—not bad for someone who had just turned twenty-five.

* * *

IN 2009, THE US NATIONAL CHAMPIONSHIPS TOOK PLACE in Indianapolis, where Aaron had qualified for his first Olympic team in 2000. That year, the neoprene competition suit stirred a controversy, as swimmers were post-ing unbelievably fast times out of nowhere. More than two hundred world records were set that year, before the suits came under scrutiny and were eventually banned. Aaron also signed a new sponsorship contract around that time, switching from Nike[89] to Arena, an Italian swimwear and clothing manufacturer.

Wella and Tim, of course, hoped Aaron would make the World Cham-pionships to be held in Rome. They cheered him on at the trials, as he won both the 100- and 200-meter backstroke events, even setting a new world record in the 100-meter. Having lunch with them one day, Aaron mentioned that he wanted them to go to Rome. Tim demurred, since it was not in their budget at the time. But Aaron insisted, saying he meant to treat them and would plan the whole trip. Wella and Tim were astonished.

The upside for Aaron was having his family there to watch him swim.

"After all they put in for me to go to practice, that ultimately led to me being able to pay for them to enjoy Rome," Aaron explains. He acknowledg-es now the growth in himself over countless meets, going from the "Why are you here?" teen snarkiness of earlier competitions to a new stage, where he says instead, "Come with me."

"Strange how it's come full circle," he observes. That, he emphasizes, is a triumph.

"Looking back, we wonder if he had been considering leaving the sport and this was a grand good-bye, in a sense," Tim remarks.

However, they were thrilled to go, as they'd never been to Rome. Aaron booked a room for them at the Grand Hotel de la Minerve, fifty yards from the Pantheon and minutes from the Trevi Fountain, Piazza Navona, and the Spanish Steps. The elegant five-star hotel—featuring graceful arches, frescoed ceilings, and a stained-glass atrium in the lobby—was once a magnificent mansion built in the 1600s. Now modernized, it is gloriously aristocratic.

"We felt like royalty as we opened our shutters to the bustling area around the Pantheon," recalls Tim.

Aaron characteristically breezed through the preliminaries for the 100-meter backstroke, and the semi-finals were scheduled for the evening. In between the races, Wella and Tim went to meet the sponsors at the Arena lounge, where family members could relax and get snacks. There they met the CEO of Arena, Cristiano Portas, whom they asked about swimming fa-cilities in Rome where they might be able to get in their customary workouts.

"Within ten minutes, we were being driven by private car to an area where Arena had their products displayed for the public and being outfitted in everything from suits to goggles, towels, and bathrobes," Tim remembers. From there, they were driven to a private facility that was slated to open in a few days: There were two 50-meter pools, one indoors and another outdoors, and "any workout machinery known to man. We were treated like royalty and met a man named Stefano who made it known we were welcome any day, any time, as his personal guests."

"It was just *beautiful*," Wella says of the facility. "We have never seen a more spectacular pool—with palm trees planted all around."

Feeling refreshed by their workout and confident that Aaron would nail his semi-finals, since he'd recently broken his own world record at Nationals, Wella and Tim returned for the race that evening. While it is not unusual for the top seed to hold back a bit in the semi-finals, Aaron miscalculated and landed in ninth place overall, one place out of the finals—a crushing outcome for the best backstroker in the world, Tim emphasizes. Wella and Tim, utterly deflated and unable to talk to Aaron, left the meet.

They woke up the next day still disheartened, but Aaron called and asked to come visit them at the hotel.

"This *never* happens at big meets; we never see him and rarely even get to talk to him," Tim says. "He was coming over to let us know he was all right and, more specifically, to make sure his mom was all right. He is well aware of how hard this was on her, not because he had let her down, but because he knows how Wella bleeds in every way for the children and their ultimate happiness. We had a great visit and Aaron made us feel better and began the process of thinking about the next swim."

Aaron didn't repeat his mistake in the 200-meter events. He handily navigated the prelims and semis. The final would pit him against his opponent, Ryan Lochte, and the Japanese sensation Ryosuke Irie. Aaron not only won the final, he also set a new world record, becoming the first man to post a time of less than 1:52.00 in the event.

"The sad thoughts and emotions of the past days swept away, and we were hugging and kissing anyone we could find," says Tim. Cristiano, Arena's CEO, sent two beefy "warehouse managers" (personal security, as far as Tim and Wella could tell) to bring them down to the poolside. They were planted in the stadium's front row, where the athletes who had medaled would parade past. After the ceremony, the medalists began their victory lap, and Aaron heard their yells and stopped for a hug and "some big tears from

Mom and Dad," according to Tim. Photographers were clicking away, and some of those photos captured the raw emotions of parents who were truly proud and happy for their son.

The cherry on the sundae was the gold medal in the final event of the meet, when Aaron and his US teammates set a world record in the 4x100-meter medley relay.

To Wella's and Tim's surprise, Aaron called after the meet with a request to go sightseeing. "We did a great group tour of the Vatican and had fun hanging out with our son," Tim recalls. "The trip couldn't have ended any better, and we were so proud of how Aaron handled the emotions of a meet where adversity reared its head."

Chapter 13 : Willpower

Wella's Tips for Staying Afloat: *Some people think they can drive their kids to succeed, but it won't work. I was super fortunate in that I put my kids into something they happened to excel at. As Tim says, What odds!*

THE MOST POIGNANT PART OF PARENTING IS THAT, despite all the hardships and sacrifice, you pour heart and soul into loving children who ultimately have to grow independent of you. You have to give them up.

As any mother knows, that is not easy. If you are like Wella, you might be even more sensitive than most. She had shielded her kids from dire financial situations, from hurtful rivalries—and from her own mistakes. The fact that she managed to pay off her debts and raise children who became exceptionally successful is a noteworthy feat. The difficulties she encountered only forged in her a stronger desire to keep Aaron and Hayley from harm. So it has been a challenge for her to watch as they grow into full-fledged adults whom she can no longer protect.

Aaron describes his mother with admiration: "I feel some people may go through life with their guard up and never let themselves go to love. My mother loves unconditionally and very deeply, in a way that is a model for how I would like to love. She is incredibly insightful and has a way of making sense of the world that is essential to me as a son. Mom has unwavering values that are easy to identify over time; she is honest, up-front, fair, active, and caring. She is sensitive yet strong-willed."

Stacey Zapolski, the Peirsol kids' first coach, also has glowing words about Wella's mothering. "As a mom, I believe there is value in friendships made with other moms who are farther down the path of motherhood. Wella has been one of these moms for me," Zapolski reveals. "While our daily lives have not crossed since the YMCA days back in 1990–91, I have enjoyed having phone conversations and seeing her many times over the years. She is a role model for me, as her children are role models for my children. I tell Wella often that her kids are great swimmers, but more importantly, they are even better people.

"Wella has been able to support her children without becoming demanding of athletic excellence," Zapolski continues. "This is easier said than done, as it is easy for parents to live vicariously though their children. Wella was able to realize as a young mom that her children's athletic successes or failures were never a reflection on her success as a mom. Her success was based upon providing a loving and nurturing environment that allowed Aaron and Hayley to flourish."[90]

Wella set out on her own with big aspirations for her children. She clung tenaciously to those dreams and never wavered in her resolve. With little money or support, and no one to believe in her at the start, she made a place for her children in a respectable community and reinforced their self-esteem by teaching them discipline and extremely hard work. She believed whole-heartedly in their abilities and loved them unconditionally, and the payoff seems miraculous.

From the time Aaron was eleven years old, Wella confided to Tim her hopes for her kids' swimming success. In what Tim likens to a "reality distortion field"—a term coined by Steve Jobs's associates, in reference to his confidence about implementing his far-fetched notions—Wella, without telling Aaron or Hayley, kept that positive mental image in mind for years. She almost *willed* them to succeed.

Similarly, what propelled Aaron throughout his long career was focusing on the big picture instead of letting losses along the way bring him down. The coaches and Wella and Tim had recognized all along how comfortable Aaron was with himself. He knew what he wanted and had the quiet confidence that he would achieve it.

Performance coach Doug Newburg wrote about an interview with Aaron on his blog:[91] "Aaron's journey to Olympic Gold started on the beaches of Southern California, playing in the water, where he learned to feel comfortable, to discover what was natural, 'just a feeling' he gets that is 'beyond words.' His love of the water led him to competitive swimming, which offered a natural structure of progress, defined not by winning and losing, but doing things his way, patiently chasing world records, emulating other swimmers he looked up to.

"Aaron's perspective, his love of the water, his understanding of himself allowed him to make the choice freely to go through that wall, to move from playing to performing."

In February 2011, on early-morning sports talk radio, Coach Eddie Reese announced Aaron's retirement from swimming. Aaron was twenty-seven years old. He had been contemplating retirement for at least a year, probably even since arranging the special accommodations for Wella and Tim at the World Championships in Rome in 2009. He leaves the sport with a trail of wins that seems superhuman. As he has pointed out in post-retirement interviews on the subject, he accomplished everything he set out to do. Not only that, he made it through twenty years of competition with a virtually untarnished reputation as a good human being. He has used his power wisely and for good causes.

Aaron's last major competition, the Pan Pacific Championships in August 2010, took place in Irvine, California, in the very place he began training with Coaches Brian Pajer and Dave Salo at Novaquatics—under the sunny skies and eucalyptus trees of Southern California at the William Woollett Jr. Aquatics Center.

Coming off tremendous success seems like it might offer Aaron a new lease on life. His first move was to drive cross-country with his dogs on a trip he had dreamed of for years. He visited friends and family, including his stepsister Erin's family and his grandmother, in her nineties.

* * *

HAYLEY MADE HEADLINES IN 2009 WITH HER SWITCH TO THE SPORT of triathlon, winning second place at her first professional ITU[92] race (a triathlon series for world-class triathletes) in Austin, Texas, where Aaron lived. She was training under Siri Lindley in harsh conditions and learning to ride steep climbs in the hot, arid climate of Borrego Springs, California. Her performances elicited yelps of excitement from spectators and commentators at a number of triathlons as she sliced through the water, leaving other racers to wallow in her bubbles during the swim portion of the events. Privately, she struggled with ambivalence about triathlons, complaining to her family that many triathletes talk only about times and training. Then, after a couple of bad falls off the bike when no one stopped to help, and a few other disillusionments, she walked away in 2011.

She began teaching swim lessons at posh homes in Los Angeles and Malibu, earning affection and flowers from her young charges, then drifted north to room with an old swim friend.

It was time to move on.

* * *

IN DECEMBER 2011, GREG HARTIG GOT MARRIED, and the whole family reunited for the first time in years, in Southern California. Tim said getting all the kids together again was something that had been "on his bucket list." It was priceless watching, for example, Aaron and Erin talking on the side of the dance floor, each with an arm draped around the other.

* * *

ONE OF THE FASCINATING THINGS ABOUT THIS STORY IS how new scientific studies back up the choices Wella made about exercise. Exercise's effects on the body are well documented. Clearly, it strengthens muscles and the cardiovascular system, and the endorphins released by intense exercise even have a colloquial name: "runner's high." But only recently have scientists begun to untangle the complicated biochemistry of how exercise affects the brain and how imperative it is that human beings keep moving.

So how was it, precisely, that Wella's decision to exercise made such a difference in the course of her life and in the lives of her children?

This isn't a lesson you slept through in biology class. It is a hot topic in neurology circles, and only in the last few years has some of the discussion come to light in articles written for the general public.[93]

Neuroscientists have found that exercise actually spurs the production of new cells (a process called *neurogenesis*) and of neurochemicals (chemical messengers) in the brain that essentially reverse the detrimental effects of stress and depression. Ongoing exercise literally helps the brain to grow and nudges neurons to connect via growing branches, enhancing the brain's ability to function. Even at the cellular and genetic level, scientists are finding indications that physical activity stimulates the brain. Proteins produced by muscle movement travel to the brain—to play roles as insulin-like growth factor 1 (IGF-1) and vascular endothelial growth factor (VEFG), which facilitate learning. Instead of being hardwired, as biologists once envisioned, the brain seems to be constantly rewiring itself, taking cues from each individual's circumstances and environment. Exercise creates new neurons, and an enriched environment helps those neurons thrive.

In fact, author Dr. John Ratey writes, "Your life changes when you have a working knowledge of your brain. It takes guilt out of the equation when you recognize that there's a biological basis for certain emotional issues. On the other hand, you won't be left feeling helpless when you see how you can influence that biology."[94]

Unrelieved stress and anxiety literally damage the brain at a cellular level, by rupturing cells. In a person with no outlet for frustration and no sense of control, the branching neurons in the brain retract. Without the flow of growth factor and serotonin, no replacement cells are generated to continue the brain's growth. There are no new stem cells to turn into neurons, leading to a scarcity of neural pathways by which to reroute anxiety, creating a downward spiral toward chronic anxiety and depression.

Despite that grim scenario, studies show that we also have the capacity to rejigger our state of mind. "After all," writes Ratey, "the purpose of the fight-or-flight response is to mobilize us to act, so physical activity is the natural way to prevent the negative consequences of stress. When we exercise in response to stress, we're doing what human beings have evolved to do over the past several million years."[95]

So when Wella first starting jogging up the beach, she was doing exactly what she needed to do to turn around the circumstances of her life.

Genetics play a part in how you cope with stress, as does individual experience. Chronic, unrelieved stress damages your brain, whereas actively coping with that stress moves you out of dangerous mental territory. Anyone who takes a walk or a run at lunch when pressure is building recognizes the truth of this premise.

When the level of stress triggers the body's production of norepinephrine (heightened alert) and dopamine (focus), the brain kicks into gear.[96] Afterward, the "high" may be from the level of serotonin (the feel-good chemical). It's that old fight-or-flight motivation, adapting to a modern world. Despite our fairly tame, technological society, our biology hasn't outgrown the need for stimulation. Our biological reaction to stress helps explain why stress junkies seek danger and why some ADHD patients seemed wired to instigate a commotion—or why exercise addicts might push their limits in extreme sports.

We are amazingly complex beings, and many variables, from genetics to biochemistry to environmental factors, make it exceedingly tricky to tease out general principles that apply to all of us.

Parents today have to negotiate balance not only in traditional ways, but in the proliferation of really cool technology. The possibilities of this new era seem nothing short of magic. We connect with people globally, without so much as a few seconds' delay. Instant messaging and cell phones have knitted humanity together in ways we never even dreamed before, giving rise to populist movements as diverse as the upending of the publishing world by bloggers and the political changes wrought by the dramatic Arab Spring.

However, there is a disconnect in our wired society. Human biology has not completed its metamorphosis to fit our digital future. Our brains and our bodies *require* physical activity, making it even more imperative that we tend to our health. The American population is struggling to understand the escalating prevalence of mental-health issues such as attention-deficit hyperactivity disorder (ADHD) and depression, increasing incidence of autoimmune disorders, and childhood obesity. Meanwhile, physical education in public schools has been sidelined by districts looking for ways to trim their budgets, and growing numbers of kids are plugged in to computers or smartphones and skipping the kickball.

Families who do recognize the need for physical activity may find a dearth of pick-up games in the neighborhood, often replaced by competitive club sports peppered across suburbia. Among young adults, extreme sports (so called because of the high level of inherent danger) have burgeoned, catering to people bursting out of their work cubicles with the desire to live a fulfilling existence. Perhaps the growing ranks of triathletes train to compensate for the physical challenges that have been sucked out of modern daily life.

These are all issues correlated with an increase in sedentary lifestyles. For all its magic, technology has essentially benched many of us from the physical labor and play that we are biologically designed to do. No longer are we farmers; no longer do our children run and ride bikes from dawn until dinner. In a culture where few of us are still breaking broncos, swinging sledgehammers, or throwing hay bales to earn our keep, we now sit in air-conditioned offices and work on glowing screens, shuttled about in cars. Our bodies and brains may not have accepted or adapted to these adjustments just yet.

When you consider the implications of reduced physical activity, then, it becomes clear that some of the body's most vital chemicals—our natural pain killers, mood enhancers, and messengers for cell regeneration—are at risk in today's society.

One can't simply pick up neurotransmitters and opioids at Walgreens. Those chemicals are a complex primordial stew concocted of sunlight, nutrition, and exercise.

When Wella began to run, then to swim, she got those juices flowing to center herself. Once she established her exercise routine, she worked up the courage to become a single parent for a time, trying—like so many of us—to do right by her children. She had big dreams for them from the start, dreams she never relinquished. Though she struggled financially, she found a job that fed her kids yet allowed her to pick them up after school and take them to swim practice. When she and Tim met, they had to sort through complicated past lives, with a blended family and children who did not necessarily have the same interests, strengths, or temperaments.

Wella points out that she and Tim would not be the people they are today, if they had not continued to exercise through all the ups and downs.

Despite the odds, this family launched a spectacular rise to the highest echelons of swimming. As Wella faced down serious anxieties and emotional and financial deficits, she discovered the power of physical exertion to heal, and she pursued that avenue for herself and her kids with gutsy resolve. While not all of us will end up on the Olympic blocks, hers is a clear lesson: We have the power to change our own lives.

Wella's tale and the remarkable success of her children underscore the interconnectedness of exercise, family, and mental well-being. Focusing on the positive and setting personal goals can be powerful. Sensible eating and exercise seem too simple a prescription to have to write, but the proof is in the pool. Or on the trail.

In the end, all it took was water and willpower.

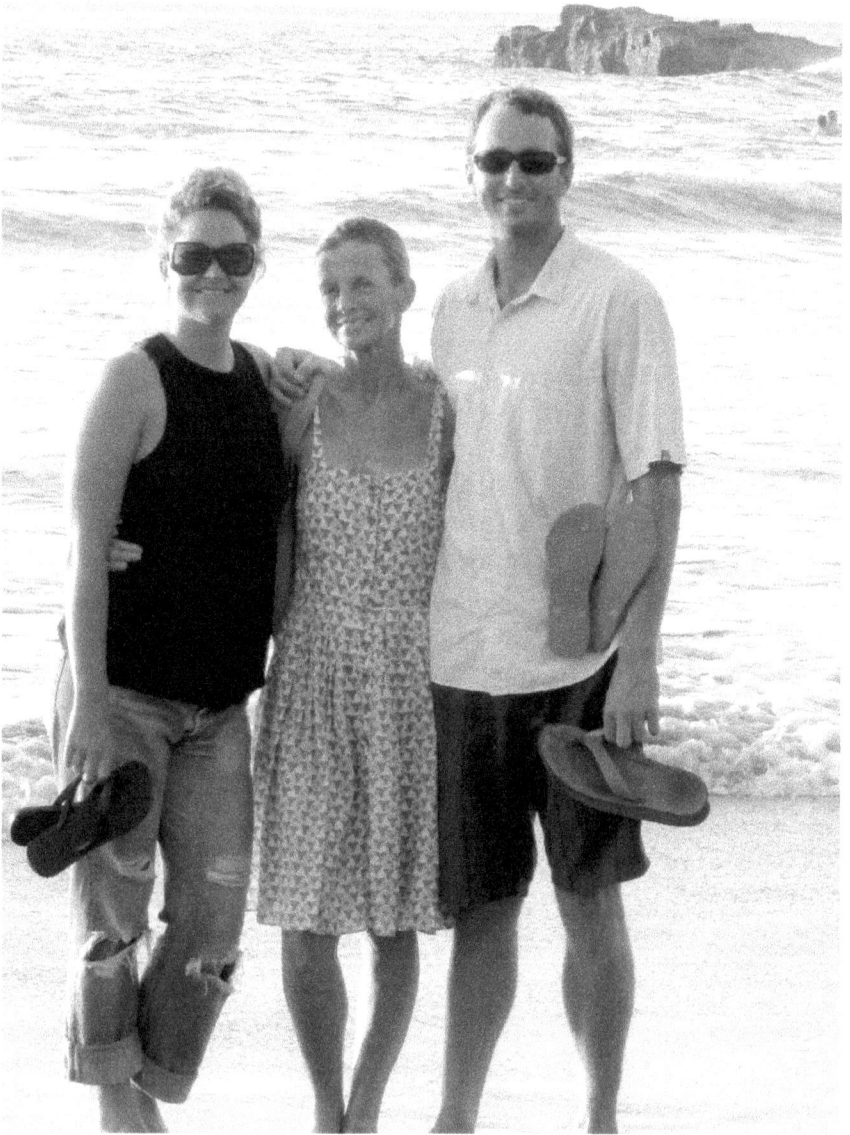

Hayley, Wella, and Aaron in 2012.
PHOTO COURTESY OF WELLA HARTIG

Chapter 14 : Balance

Wella's Tip for Staying Afloat: *In the whole scheme of life, 'it's just one race,' as Dave Salo says. There are other things more important.*

BERKELEY HUMS WITH BUSES, THE HEAVY UNDERGROUND RATTLE of Bay Area Rapid Transit, and snippets of conversation in every possible language. Houses and apartments are stacked along side streets and perched on steep hilltops overlooking the eucalyptus forest on the Cal Berkeley campus. The cultural milieu here is a far cry from the tidy, tree-lined boulevards in Orange County.

Hayley—wearing a gray cowl-necked sweatshirt over athletic attire and stylishly large, brown-tinted sunglasses—relaxes at a patio table with a bowl-sized almond-milk cappuccino one sunny September morning. She is totally energized by the program she has just started, a three-year course that trains teachers for Waldorf schools. Her first few days in the program have been refreshing. "It is fantastic to be around a group of people you can talk to about your interests. So now it's like I am actually a part of something totally different, for different reasons. I am coming together with people where I am now," she says.

In a fascinating parallel to her mother at a similar age, Hayley found her new course in life by reading. She describes being distracted on long training (bike) rides, a sense of craving to read and learn instead of train, and she found she was no longer focused on triathlon. Turned on to Hermann Hesse's *Siddhartha* by an ex-boyfriend from Tunisia, she followed up on the author's reference to another text. Soon, she was immersed in Emerson and Thoreau, as well.

"Every second I had to myself, I would read," Hayley recalls of a period during her triathlon training when she came across one book after another that seemed to speak directly to her. "It was amazing because I felt like I was no longer lost or alone." Putting into action the saying that recommends one put to good use what others write, Hayley cross-referenced transcendentalism with some other ideas she was batting about, and discovered the nearby teacher-training program for Waldorf.

The Waldorf approach to education is based on the philosophy of Rudolf Steiner of Austria. The program emphasizes interdisciplinary learning and the role of the imagination in learning, aiming to develop thinking that is both creative and analytical. The Waldorf goal is to assist with the development of "free, morally responsible and integrated individuals, and to help every child fulfill his or her unique destiny."[97]

"I look at athletics differently today," Hayley says. "The emphasis is on competition, time, numbers. I find that, when you're done with that, it has taught you responsibility. But it's also a disservice because of too much emphasis on competition. When I was young, if I had a coach I trusted, I loved to work hard. I did well because of that. Only about six months ago did I realize how talented I was."

Now that she is coaching "overachievers' kids" in just one small part of California, she recognizes the level and breadth of competition she must have beat when she was younger and qualified for Junior Olympics, NCAAs, and Olympic Trials.

"But it was all I knew. So how can you gain perspective in the middle of it?" She laughs and then speculates, "If I'd actually had *goals*… Imagine!"

In college at Auburn, the swimmers roomed together. They lived two houses apart, at most. She says that was the beauty of a small school, that the team was super close. However, she notes, "no one stays in Alabama." Her friends fanned out across the country after college, and she found it was like losing five years of family when they were suddenly not together anymore.

"My priorities in college were athletics," she explains. "I wasn't even using that other part of my brain. Towards the end of triathlon, it was almost like the side of me that had been lying dormant was starting to develop. While I was riding, practicing, I wanted to be reading, studying."

Hayley is also grateful she had a chance to try a different sport as a young adult, because, in her words, "it was, like, super humbling. I was number three in the world in swimming but then got thrown in with the triathletes. The bike was hard. I rushed into it so fast. I crashed all the time, just didn't have the opportunity to build confidence. I think I did two or three amateur races and then—off to Europe, racing these crazy courses. I didn't know how to fix my bike, didn't know the lingo."

There was definitely a bump as she transitioned out of professional sports. Wella fretted because Hayley went through a dark period, casting about for direction after she left triathlon training. "I told my mom it would be bad if everything was always good," she comments dryly, adding that ex-athletes probably need rehabilitation. Elite athletes have spent so much time in disciplined, regular practice; then, suddenly, time stretches empty before them. "Only when you've experienced it can you know how debilitating it feels… but you have to sit alone with yourself, listen to your inner voice" to find a new direction, she counsels.

Hayley still has a foot in the world of athletics. Her roommate and best friend, Kim Vandenberg, competed at Olympic Trials in August 2012; plus, Hayley has been coaching in a nearby aquatics program, one she believes is similar to Nova, in terms of philosophy. The swim program focuses on character; the push is not just about going fast but about giving kids the skills and tools to have a long swimming career. On the team website, an anonymous quotation affirms, "Prepare the child for the path, not the path for the child." She says it is considered among the best club teams in Northern California.

"I am coaching seven- to fourteen-year-olds," Hayley explains. "I love that age, though I am leaning toward teaching younger ones, kindergarten or first grade. *That* age has no inhibitions. They just do things because they want to do them. They don't know how not to be in the present. I love that! It puts things into such amazing perspective. It always makes whatever I'm dealing with better. It reminds me not to get so stuck in my petty issues."

"Hayley didn't love swimming the way I did," Aaron observes. "She found a love for it but realized she should move on sooner. I am happy she did, as she was going against the grain."

Aaron warns not to underestimate how import the camaraderie was for Hayley—maybe that is what she loved most, the social aspect of sports. That may have meant the difference: Perhaps it was because she did not have the Olympics as a real goal.

"The Olympics are great, but you have to work hard for it, be chosen, and be willing to do what it takes," Aaron emphasizes. "If you're not doing it for the right reasons, it can cause damage. You need to ask yourself—Are you having a good time?"

An elegant new Olympians Plaza, installed the Texas Swim Center in Austin, circles a grove of trees with medallions that show every Olympian who has passed through the University of Texas swimming and diving

AARON PEIRSOL

Backstroke

"A first-class statesman for the sport of swimming."

2000 2004 2008

program. Among the eighty so far are some recognizable names, but Aaron Peirsol has an impressive record, even among the stars. The plaque designated for him denotes his five gold and two silver medals. The inscribed phrase deems Aaron "A first-class statesman for the sport of swimming." His two world records still stand, despite the hype surrounding certain swimmers at the 2012 Summer Olympics.

"Yet Aaron has never done these things for the medals," Wella points out. In his house, there are no indicators of his success, except a photo of him alongside Jason Lezak, Brendan Hansen, and Ian Crocker, who were on the relay with him in Athens. "Someone took a photo of the back of their heads, as they were lined up in their sweats, ready to be announced. In front of them is the billboard with USA in the middle."

For Aaron, swimming may have been a little bit about camaraderie, too. And a lot about his love for the water. On a recent trip to South Africa to teach a swim clinic, he came across a quote written on a wooden bench on Jeffreys Beach:[98] "The sun's mirror has a salt that sweetens the soul," a reference to the ocean.

"The people who wrote that quote, they get it," he says, leaning back and nodding. "It's intrinsic—doesn't need much explanation. A cool little pleasure."

Acknowledgments

WITHOUT THE GRACIOUS ASSISTANCE OF AARON AND HAYLEY,
this book would have been difficult to complete. On a sweltering July day,
Aaron moved an entire storage shed of heavy containers to find a few specific
family photos. On a busy weekend after she had started new classes, Hayley
explained eloquently the double-edged sword of athletic success. Both of
them opened up their lives, at a time when they fully deserve privacy, and
contributed insights and anecdotes that made the narrative infinitely stronger. Erin Hartig and Greg Hartig, too, deserve recognition and admiration
for sharing honest answers and very personal memories. Special thanks to
all the coaches who generously answered questions, explained the inner
workings of the sport of swimming, and shared anecdotes that illustrated
their side of this story. All these perspectives helped illuminate the picture
of this blended family and authenticated Wella's and Tim's memories of
circumstances.

Certain folks went out of their way to contribute unique details to the
book: Dr. D'Anna Adkins; Dr. Tracy Greer; Dr. Larry Cottam; Dr. Leigh
Leasure; Vivienne Van de Voorde; Michele Mullen; Deborah Thompson,
librarian at Brenau University; TerryLynn Fisher, Ben Blank, and John Harkins at the Orange County District Attorney's Office; and Patricia at Stacey
Pool, with her comment that opened the door for an important friendship.
And without the great neighborhood and municipal pools in Austin, we
lap-swimmers never would have met.

Many talented people contributed their efforts to shepherd this story
to light. Among the staunchest supporters are Colleen Hobbs; the Austin
BIO crew—Ann Rowe Seaman, PJ Pierce, Alison Macor, Bill Crawford, and
Laura Castro; the WednesDivas—PJ Pierce, Mary Day Long, Jeanne Guy,
Debra Winegarten, and Marty McAllister; our brilliant copyeditor, Aaron
Hierholzer; our talented cover and book designer, Gloria Lee; wise col-
leagues at Austin SCBWI; assistant sleuth and photographer extraordinaire
Gretchen Robbins; and our early and enthusiastic readers Melinda Gesuale,
Melanie and Larry Cottam, Fleur Smithpeter, Amy Simpson, Susie Morri-
son, and Leigh Hopper. Many thanks to advisors Kim Allen, Cathy Finley,
Wendy Walsh, Janell Cottam, Liz Peña, Peg McCoy, and Germaine Curry.
We are also much indebted for professional advice from Nicholas Lemann,
Bill Minutaglio; Dr. James Ragan, Bruce Selcraig, and Bill Crawford. Thank
you to the savvy team at Firebrand (a.k.a. eBook Architects), particularly the

ingenious Joshua Tallent.

We cannot overstate our love and appreciation for Tim Hartig and Greg Sajbel, who have provided rock-solid support, encouraging us at every turn of this adventure. Thank you, guys.

Swim fast!

Wella and Laura

Notes

[1] *Wikipedia,* s.v. "Irvine, California," http://en.wikipedia.org/wiki/City_of_Irvine.

[2] Press release from *USA Triathlon* magazine, issued November 2009.

[3] In swimming, world records are maintained and verified by FINA, the Fédération Internationale de Natation Amateur in Lausanne, Switzerland. FINA is recognized by the International Olympic Committee as the organization authorized to oversee international competition in aquatic sports. Official records are also maintained at USA Swimming, headquartered in Colorado.

[4] Interview with Eddie Reese, November 30, 2010.

[5] Officially named Sunkist Growers, Incorporated. This is a non-stock membership cooperative composed of members in California and Arizona. Begun as the Southern California Fruit Exchange in Claremont in 1893, renamed in 1905 as the California Fruit Growers Exchange, it adopted three years later the "Sunkist" name for its top-quality oranges, becoming the first company to brand fruit.

[6] Dennis McLellan, "Larry Capune, 61, Traveled Thousands of Miles on Solo Paddleboard Odysseys," *Los Angeles Times,* June 6, 2004.

[7] "Wella Peirsol Hartig: Mom of 2 Olympic-Level Athletes Advises Parents Not to Pressure Kids To Succeed in Sports," MomsTeam.com, May 1, 2012, http://www.momsteam.com/blog/may-sports-moms-month/wella-peirsol-hartig-being-mom-2-olympic-athletes-says-no-pressure-on-kids-to-succeed#ixzz2OtcB0vSC.

[8] Video about Sammy Lee made by NBC in 1998, International Swimming Hall of Fame video archives, Fort Lauderdale, Florida; also, USAdiving.com website interview of Sammy Lee.

[9] Yearbook pages of Bebe Wells, scanned by Brenau University librarian Deborah Thompson, acquired March 22, 2012. Brenau was a women's college until 1992, when it became a university. Bebe's background was mentioned in interviews with family and listed in an "Aaron Peirsol" genealogy at http://freepages.genealogy.rootsweb.ancestry.com/~battle/olympics08/peirsol.htm.

[10] A number of current studies about the effects of exercise on the brain are neatly chronicled in *Spark: The Revolutionary New Science of Exercise and the Brain,* by John R. Ratey and Eric Hagerman (New York: Little, Brown, 2008).

[11] Those roses still grow in the yards at the houses where Wella lived, per

research trip in October 2011.

[12] Ratey and Hagerman, *Spark, 101–103.*

[13] Luxury apartments where the Peirsols lived by that point in Newport Beach, just up the hill from Balboa Island.

[14] According to *Wikipedia,* American swimmer Mark Spitz won seven gold medals in the 1972 Olympics, in Munich, Germany. Between 1968 and 1972, he won a total of nine Olympic golds, a silver, and a bronze, as well as many other swimming awards and titles. He set thirty-three world records in swimming over the course of his career.

[15] Wella and Tim showed the coauthor one of Aaron's swim-record books, published by California Swimming, in which he had handwritten in red pen his name and his own record-breaking time over the previous record. Hayley had also written her name on the page that listed her races.

[16] Officially, it is called Upper Newport Bay.

[17] From conversations and follow-up e-mails written by Stacey Zapolski, November 15, 2010, and December 2, 2011

[18] David Shenk, *The Genius in All of Us: New Insights into Genetics, Talent, and IQ* (New York: Anchor Books, 2011), 120.

[19] Junior Olympics is a series of prestigious regional meets for young swimmers who finish in first, second, or third place at sanctioned swimming championships. More information about qualifying standards at http://www.usaswimming.org/DesktopDefault.aspx or at http://www.usaswimming.org/DesktopDefault.aspx.

[20] California Junior Guard webpage at http://www.jrlifeguards.com/jgpage1.html.

[21] Gearing up for a trial, a lawyer procured a copy of the letter for Tim and Wella.

[22] According to the official Old Orange County Courthouse website, http://www.ocparks.com/oldcourthouse/, accessed May 21, 2012.

[23] A permanent plaque inside the aquatics center details the history of the pool.

[24] E-mail interview with Brian Pajer, December 16, 2010

[25] Erik Hamilton reported on sports and Orange County as a staff writer for the *Los Angeles Times* from 1991–2002, according to archived articles.

[26] Phone conversation and e-mail interview with Brian Pajer, December 16, 2010.

[27] Interview with Coach Dave Salo, October 26, 2011.

[28] Phone call to Southern California Swimming, March 18, 2013. One of

fifty-nine local swimming committees under the auspices of USA Swimming, SCS oversees official swim times and regulations in accordance with the standards, rules, regulations, policies, and procedures of Fédération Internationale de Natation Amateur (FINA), United States Swimming, Inc. (USA Swimming), and SCS, according to its website: www.socalswim.org/mission.aspx.

[29] USA Swimming is the national governing body that oversees official swim times and regulations in accordance with the standards, rules, regulations, policies and procedures of Fédération Internationale de Natation Amateur (FINA) and United States Swimming, Inc. (USA Swimming). Promotes the sport of swimming for members from age-level groups to Olympic teams, as well as coaches and volunteers: http://www.usaswimming.org/DesktopDefault.aspx?TabId=1412&Alias=Rainbow&Lang=en.

[30] USA Swimming archives.

[31] Interview with Hayley Peirsol, September 9, 2012.

[32] Shenk, *Genius*, 67.

[33] From www.si-swimming.com/?p=2007: "Junior Olympic time standards are set locally here in San Diego and are recomputed annually to select approximately the 24 fastest swimmers in each event based upon the average results for the event over the past 3–5 years. These time standards can, and often do, change by small amounts from year to year in order to keep up with advances (and sometimes declines) in the various age/gender groups."

[34] Date confirmed on document titled "Agreement for Release on Own Recognizance," issued by Superior Court of the State of California for the County of Orange, signed by Mary L. Peirsol and Witness #633.

[35] Business card information verified by Terry Lynn Fisher at the Orange County District Attorney's office, who conferred with Ben Blank and John Harkins to determine accuracy for business cards, badges, and circumstances for 1993–94. In 1995, the cards were changed to protect client confidentiality, and "welfare" was divided into categories and renamed ("CalWorks"). Phone conversations and e-mails from April 6–8, 2011.

[36] According to Felony Complaint-Criminal #94HF0539, filed in Orange County Superior Court on September 22, 1994, earlier received in Municipal Court on July 22, 1994, subscribed and sworn on July 13, 1994, by Michael Capizzi, district attorney of Orange County, California.

[37] Court documents indicate proceedings began August 18, 1994, with Craig E. Robison presiding, and attorney Michael Doudna as Mary Louella Peirsol's representative.

[38] Guilty plea in the Superior Court (County of Orange County), filed and signed September 22, 1994.

[39] "I was really, really naïve. I had no idea it would be a felony," Wella says. Fraud involving an amount over $400 is a major crime, punishable by a minimum of a year in prison in most cases. With court costs, interest, and penalties, the amount Wella owed had escalated.

[40] Minute Order: "People vs. Peirsol, Mary Louella," entered September 22, 1994.

[41] Dates, names, charges, pleas, addresses, probation and sentencing, and other case information drawn from original documents obtained from the Central Justice Center at 700 Civic Center Drive in Santa Ana, through the Criminal Records clerk, October 26, 2011.

[42] Wella recalls exactly what she wore to be booked; Skype conversation, March 8, 2012.

[43] Superior Court of the State of California for the County of Orange, Minute Order, dated January 20, 1995.

[44] Information confirmed in "Back to Basics" by Ingo Winzer, which appeared in the Mortgage Bankers Association newsletter *Mortgage Banking* in October 2009.

[45] Ashok Bardhan and Richard Walker, "California, Pivot of the Great Recession: Working Paper No. 20310," Institute for Research on Labor & Employment, University of California–Berkeley, March 2010. Ashok Bardhan teaches in the Fisher Center for Real Estate and Urban Economics, and Richard Walker in the Department of Geography, California Studies Center, both at Berkeley. In their paper, Bardhan and Walker declare that "more than any other place, California was the source of mass mortgage lending, ballooning home values, and dubious subprime operations," and that the state "needs to be recognized as a pivotal site of the bubble of the 2000s." The authors assert that California "banks engaged in some of the worst excesses of the housing bubble," and point out that "California boasts the largest housing sector among the fifty states and its housing is the most unaffordable—making borrowers more vulnerable and susceptible to mortgage overreach."

[46] Statistics on Irvine drawn from *Wikipedia*'s entry on the city. In 2008, Irvine ranked as seventh-richest city in the United States.

[47] Wella lists the Magellan address as hers on official court documents dated September 22, 1994. A property search lists Tim's house on Magellan as having been "foreclosed and bank-owned" and sold by June 26, 1995, http://

www.redfin.com/CA/Costa-Mesa/957-Magellan-St-92626/home/3710298.

[48] As told to Doug Newburg and posted at http://dougnewburg.com/inter-view-with-aaron-peirsol-olympic-medalist-part-1, May 2012.

[49] USA Swim records, age group times, online at http://www.usaswimming.org/DesktopDefault.aspx?TabId=1480&Alias=Rainbow&Lang=en.

[50] Hayley has preserved the signed program and the articles about Aaron and Bridgewater in a scrapbook she made as a gift for Aaron in high school.

[51] Although the date is cut off, Hayley also saved the article titled "Bridge-water in Troubled Waters" by Erik Hamilton in the scrapbook she made as a gift for Aaron.

[52] The Canadian Encyclopedia (online), s.v. "Pan American Games," http://www.thecanadianencyclopedia.com/articles/panamerican-games.

[53] Brian Tracy, according to his website, www.briantracy.com, gives corporate seminars on leadership, selling, self-esteem, goals, strategy, creativity, and success psychology and has authored a number of books on these subjects.

[54] Phone interviews with Michele Mullen, March 27 and 29, 2012.

[55] Sean Gregory, "Keeping Afloat: For Many Olympic Athletes, Raising Money Is a Second Job," *Time, April 2, 2012, pp. 50–52.*

[56] Interview with Brian Pajer, October 2011.

[57] Information from the Sydney Olympic Park Aquatic Centre website at http://www.aquaticcentre.com.au/ and from the Sydney Olympic Park Aquatic Centre entry on *Wikipedia* (http://en.wikipedia.org/wiki/Sydney_International_Aquatic_Centre).

[58] Phone interviews with Michele Mullen, March 20, 27, and 29, 2012.

[59] *Daily Pilot, December 1, 2000.*

[60] Serotonin, a monoamine neurotransmitter found primarily in the gastrointestinal tract, platelets, and nervous system, is biochemically derived from tryptophan (found in foods such as poultry). It is linked to the regulation of mood, appetite, and sleep, as well as to some cognitive functioning (i.e., memory and learning) and vasoconstriction. Many researchers believe serotonin is a factor in anxiety and in depression, and studies are under way to determine non-pharmacological means of prevention.

[61] Kirsten Weir, "The Exercise Effect," American Psychology Association website, http://www.apa.org/monitor/2011/12/exercise.aspx.

[62] Ratey and Hagerman, *Spark, 90–110.*

[63] Current studies by teams of psychiatrists, psychologists, and neuroscientists are documenting the effects of prescribing exercise for patients with

depression. Dr. Tracy Greer, a colleague of lead researcher and psychiatrist Dr. Madhukar Trivedi, discussed a study called DOSE and another called TREAD in which patients were prescribed exercise of 16 kilocalories per kilogram of body weight per week, either as a monotherapy (DOSE) or to supplement their medications (TREAD). She says researchers were pleasantly surprised that people wanted to participate, and that the findings were encouraging, in that the participants who exercised reported improvements in the form of reduced depressive symptoms. She expressed that, realistically, we may need to use both drugs and exercise to get people to a place where they are able to maintain exercise, if they are depressed. She also emphasized that the quality of life aspects are something she is really excited about with exercise as a prescription for mental health. Where medications can have severe side effects, many of the side effects of exercise are beneficial. Interview with Tracy Greer, PhD, at UT Southwestern Medical School, Mood Disorders Research Program and Clinic in Dallas, Texas, on November 12, 2012. See http://www.ncbi.nlm.nih.gov/pubmed/12392873,

"The DOSE Study: A Clinical Trial to Examine Efficacy and Dose Response of Exercise as Treatment for Depression," Dunn AL, Trivedi MH, Kampert JB, Clark CG, Chambliss HO, Division of Research, The Cooper Institute, Dallas, Texas; http://www.ncbi.nlm.nih.gov/pubmed/21658349, *Journal of Clinical Psychiatry.* 2011 May; 72(5):677-84. doi: 10.4088/JCP.10m06743.

"Exercise as an Augmentation Treatment for Nonremitted Major Depressive Disorder: A Randomized, Parallel Dose Comparison," (TREAD study) by Trivedi MH, Greer TL, Church TS, Carmody TJ, Grannemann BD, Galper DI, Dunn AL, Earnest CP, Sunderajan P, Henley SS, Blair SN.

[64] Mayo Clinic information available in published materials about SSRI use for anxiety and depression: http://www.mayoclinic.com/health/gen-eralized-anxiety-disorder/DS00502/DSECTION=lifestyle%2Dand%2D-home%2Dremedies

as well as http://www.mayclinic.com/health/ssris/MH00066.

[65] Ratey and Hagerman, *Spark, 102–110.*

[66] Information on the Lee & Joe Jamail Texas Swim Center information found at http://www.tsc.utexas.edu/about.php.

[67] ASCA stands for American Swimming Coaches Association.

[68] Official UT Swimming information on Aaron Peirsol also found in profile of Coach Eddie Reese at http://www.texassports.com/sports/m-swim/mtt/reese_eddie00.html.

[69] E-mail from Coach Eddie Reese, November 30, 2010.

[70] Interview with Coach Eddie Reese, November 30, 2010.

[71] E-mail from Kris Kubik, December 1, 2010, and personal interview with Kris Kubik, November 30, 2010.

[72] E-mail from Kris Kubik, December 1, 2010.

[73] E-mail from Aaron Peirsol, April 30, 2011.

[74] E-mail from Eddie Reese, November 30, 2010. Reiterated at interview.

[75] "Swimming—Aaron Peirsol Bodysurfing Video," YouTube video, posted by goswim098, January 7, 2009, http://www.youtube.com/watch?v=rtMwtX-rkLHM.

[76] "Still Waters," an article written by Alex Hannaford for the February 2013 issue *Spirit Magazine* (Southwest Airlines's monthly publication), talks about the healing power of surfing. The author cites the successes of a program called Amazing Surf Adventures, based in San Luis Obispo, which caters to war veterans, children with special needs, and at-risk youth. Interviewing not only those whose lives have been turned around through the surf camps but also biologists, psychologists, and neuroscientists, the author makes the case that the combination of exercise (paddling), exhilaration (catching the wave), and meditation (the calming effect of water) provided by surfing "is good medicine for our minds and bodies" (60–65, 82–87).

[77] *Daily Pilot*, May 24, 2003, sports news item on Hayley Peirsol by Steve Virgen.

[78] FINA is the acronym for Fédération Internationale de Natation Amateur, based in Lausanne, Switzerland. It is the governing body recognized by the International Olympic Committee as responsible for overseeing sanctioned aquatic sports times and events.

[79] Steve Virgen, "Peirsol Renews Passion in Triathlon," *Daily Pilot*, September 4, 2008.

[80] "Peirsol Defends Title," *Daily Pilot*, March 11, 2007.

[81] *Wikipedia, s.v.* "World record progression 200 metres backstroke," http://en.wikipedia.org/wiki/World_record_progression_200_metres_backstroke

[82] "Bobby Brewer Joins PMG Sports Marketing Agency," *Swimming World* magazine's Lane 9 News Archive, July 30, 2002.

[83] Mark Fainaru-Wada, "Pool of Utter Mix-Ups: Peirsol at First DQ'd, Then Given the Gold," *San Franciso Chronicle*, August 20, 2004.

[84] "Markus Rogan Wins Silver Medal in 100 Back at Olympics," August 18, 2004, www.gostanford.com/sports/m-swim/spec-rel/081804aad.html.

[85] *Houston Chronicle* writer Fran Blinebury notes that the "olive wreath . . . dates back to the tradition of the ancient Olympics. . . . According to the

myth, Hercules brought an olive tree from his homeland . . . and planted it at the site of the first Games . . . then presented the winners of the first Games with an olive wreath." (http://www.chron.com/sports/olympics/article/Olympic-Blog-All-Greek-to-us-1520254.php#page-4).

[86] Brent Shaver, "Local Siblings' Rivalry of the Best Kind at Meet," *Orange County Register*, August 10, 2006.

[87] Ibid.

[88] Eli Saslow, "Siblings Swimming Toward the Olympics," *Washington Post,* August 3, 2006.

[89] Nike bowed out of sponsoring swimming around that time period.

[90] E-mail from Stacey Zapolski, December 2, 2010.

[91] Doug Newburg's interview of Aaron, May 2012, http://www.dougnewburg.com.

[92] ITU stands for International Triathlon Union. According to http://www.triathlon.org/, "ITU World Triathlon Series is an innovative series that allows the world's top athletes to compete head-to-head on an ongoing basis."

[93] With John Ratey's *Spark* or the February 2012 article titled "Get Outside!" by Steve Blaisdell of the *Austin American-Statesman,* or the notice in the *New York Times* in October 2000 about the study showing that exercise outperformed the drug Zoloft in treating depression.

[94] Ratey and Hagerman, *Spark, 6.*

[95] Ratey and Hagerman, *Spark, 64.*

[96] Ratey and Hagerman, *Spark, 65.*

[97] According to *Wikipedia,* as of September 2012: "Waldorf education (also known as Steiner education) is a humanistic approach to pedagogy based on the educational philosophy of the Austrian philosopher Rudolf Steiner, the founder of anthroposophy. Learning is interdisciplinary, integrating practical, artistic, and conceptual elements. . . . The . . . overarching goals are to provide young people the basis on which to develop into free, morally responsible and integrated individuals, and to help every child fulfill his or her unique destiny. . . ."

[98] Native South African Brenda Shunn confirms that this is the local name for a renowned surfing beach on Jeffreys Bay.

Selected Bibliography

INTERVIEWS

Much material has been derived from ongoing communication with family members Wella and Tim Hartig, Aaron Peirsol, and Hayley Peirsol, from 2010–2013. Only formal interviews are noted below.

Adkins, D'Anna, PhD. Interview by author. Personal interview. Austin, Texas, November 15, 2010.

Cottam, Gene Larry, PhD. Interview by author and ongoing communications. Dallas, Texas, November 11, 2012.

Greer, Tracy, PhD. Interview by author. Personal interview and ongoing email correspondence. UT Southwestern Medical Center at Dallas, November 12, 2012.

Hartig, Erin. Email correspondence with author. April 26 and May 10, 2011.

Hartig, Greg. Email correspondence with author. November 3, 2011.

Kubik, Kris. Interview by author. Personal interview. Austin. November 30, 2011.

Kubik, Kris. Email correspondence with author. December 1, 2011.

Leasure, Leigh, PhD. Interview by author. Phone interview. Austin/Houston, Texas. September 21, 2011.

Lorenzen, Brent. Interview by author. Phone interview. November 23, 2010.

Mullen, Michele. Interviews by author. Phone interview. Austin/Newport Beach, California. March 20, 27, and 29, 2012.

Pajer, Brian. Interview by author. October 26, 2011. Irvine, California.

Pajer, Brian. Email correspondence with author. October 11, 2011; December 16, 2010.

Pajer, Brian. Interview by author. Phone interview. Austin/Irvine. December 16, 2010.

Peirsol, Aaron. Interviews by author. Personal interview. May 11, 2011; also May 15, 2012.

Peirsol, Aaron. Email correspondence with author. April 30, 2011.

Peirsol, Hayley. Interview by author. Phone interview. Austin/Berkeley, California, August 17, 2012.

Peirsol, Hayley. Interview by author. Personal interview. Berkeley. September 9, 2012.

Peirsol, Hayley, Email correspondence with author. June 29, 2011.

Reese, Eddie. Email correspondence with author. November 30, 2011.

Reese, Eddie. Interview by author. Personal interview. November 30, 2011.

Salo, Dave. Interview by author. Personal interview. October 26, 2011. William Woollett Jr. Aquatics Center, Irvine, California.

Salo, Dave. Email correspondence with author. October 17, 2011.

Van de Voorde, Viviane. Interview by author. Phone interview. Austin/Chico, California. April 13, 2012.

Zapolski, Stacey. Phone interview and email correspondence with author. November 15 and December 2, 2011.

WORKS CITED

Auburn Swimming and Diving official website. http://www.auburntigers.com/sports/c-swim/aub-c-swim-body.html, accessed July 2011 through March 2013.

Archives of the *Orange Country Register*. http://www.ocregister.com/articles/archives-218862-county-orange.html, accessed May 2010 through March 2013.

Bardhan, Ashok and Richard Walker. "California, Pivot of the Great Recession: Working Paper No. 20310." Institute for Research on Labor & Employment, University of California–Berkeley. March 2010.

Barron, David, Fran Blinebury, John P. Lopez, Jonathan Feigen, Jerome Solomon. "Olympic Blog: All Greek to Us." *Houston Chronicle*. http://www.chron.com/sports/olympics/article/Olympic-Blog-All-Greek-to-us-1520254.php#page-4.

Begley, Sharon. *Train Your Mind, Change Your Brain: How a New Science Reveals Our Extraordinary Potential to Transform Ourselves*. New York: Ballantine Books, 2007.

"Blog of Death," *Los Angeles Times*, June 8, 2004.

"Beijing's Olympic Pool," by National Geographic. YouTube. Uploaded July 28, 2008. http://www.youtube.com/watch?v=7YyLwfTkL4I, accessed July 10, 2011. The building of the Beijing National Aquatics Center for the 28th Olympiad.

"Bobby Brewer Joins PMG Sports Marketing Agency." *Swimming World* magazine, Lane 9 News Archive. July 30, 2002. http://www.swimming-worldmagazine.com/lane9/news/4013.asp, accessed June 2011.

Blaisdell, Steve. "Get Outside." *Austin American-Statesman*. February 25, 2012.

California Junior Guards website. http://www.jrlifeguards.com/jgpage1.html, accessed September 2011.

Casey, Susan. *The Wave: In Pursuit of the Rogues, Freaks, and Giants of the Ocean*. New York: Doubleday, 2010.

Chansky, Tamar E., PhD, *Freeing Your Child from Anxiety: Powerful, Practical Solutions to Overcome Your Child's Fears*. New York: Three Rivers Press, Random House, 2005.

Couric, Katie. *The Best Advice I Ever Got: Lessons from Extraordinary Lives*. New York: Random House, 2011.

Cox, Lynne. *Swimming to Antarctica*. Orlando: Harcourt, 2004.

Daily Pilot archives. http://dailypilot.com, accessed May 2010 through March 2013.

Dunn, A. L., M. H. Trivedi, J. B. Kampert, C. G. Clark, and H. O. Chambliss. "The DOSE Study: A Clinical Trial to Examine Efficacy and Dose Response of Exercise as Treatment for Depression. http://www.ncbi.nlm.nih.gov/pubmed/12392873, accessed October 5, 2012.

Emmons, Henry, and Rachel Kranz. *The Chemistry of Joy: A Three-Step Program for Overcoming Depression Through Western Science and Eastern Wisdom*. New York: Simon & Schuster, 2006.

Emmons, Henry. *The Chemistry of Calm: A Powerful, Drug-free Plan to Quiet Your Fears and Overcome Your Anxiety*. New York: Simon & Schuster, 2010.

"Exercise Found Effective Against Depression." *New York Times*. October 10, 2000. http://www.nytimes.com/2000/10/10/health/exercise-found-effective-against-depression.html, accessed July 2011.

Fainaru-Wada, Mark. "Pool of Utter Mix-Ups: Peirsol at First DQ'd, Then Given the Gold." *San Francisco Chronicle*. August 20, 2004. http://www.sfgate.com/sports/article/Pool-of-utter-mix-ups-Peirsol-at-first-DQ-d-2732121.php, accessed July 2011.

"Free Public Records from the Most Updated Public Sources." http://publicrecordcenter.com, accessed August 25, 2011. Accessed public records to confirm court information prior to obtaining official copies of pertinent records.

Finn, Adharanand. *Running with the Kenyans: Discovering the Secrets of the Fastest People on Earth*. New York: Random House, 2012.

Gladwell, Malcolm. *Outliers: The Story of Success*. New York: Little, Brown, 2008.

Gregory, Sean. "Keeping Afloat: For Many Olympic Athletes, Raising Money is a Second Job." *Time*. April 20, 2012, 50–52.

Gonzalez-Wallace, Michael. *Super Body, Super Brain: The Workout That Does It All.* New York: HarperOne, 2010.

Hannaford, Alex. "Still Waters." *Spirit Magazine*, February 2013. Quotes biologists, psychologists, neuroscientists and the people whoslives have been changed by the surf camps at Amazing Surf Adventures in San Luis Obispo, California.

International Swimming Hall of Fame video archives, NBC video about Sammy Lee, made in 1998. http://www.ishof.org/video_archive/diving/sammy_lee.htm, accessed December 2010.

International Triathlon Union website. http://www.triathlon.org, accessed June 2011.

"Irvine, California," entry on *Wikipedia*, accessed October 1, 2011.

Lee and Joe Jamail Texas Swim Center website. http://www.tsc.utexas.edu/about.php,accessed October 2010.

Levine, Madeline. *The Price of Privilege: How Parental Pressure and Material Advantage Are Creating a Generation of Disconnected and Unhappy Kids.* New York: HarperCollins, 2006.

"Mark Spitz" entry on *Wikipedia*. http://en.wikipedia.org/wiki/Mark_Spitz, accessed September 2011.

"Markus Rogan Wins Silver Medal in 100 Back At Olympics," Official Website of the Stanford Cardinal, www.gostanford.com/sports/m-swim/spec-rel/081804aad.html, accessed July 2011.

McDougall, Christopher. *Born to Run: A Hidden Tribe, Superathletes, and the Greatest Race the World Has Never Seen.* New York: Alfred A. Knopf, 2009.

McLellan, Dennis. "Larry Capune, 61, Traveled Thousands of Miles on Solo Paddleboard Odysseys," *Los Angeles Times*, June 8, 2004.

"Megastructures: Beijing Water Cube," by NHNZMedia. YouTube. Uploaded on July 18, 2011. http://www.youtube.com/watch?v=x7nxl__qOJ4, accessed July 18, 2011. Referencing the Beijing National Aquatics Center, *Al Jazeera* called it a "Space Age Greenhouse." Video discusses the construction, the difficulty broadcasters faced with unusual lighting, the men's 4x100-meter medley relay where USA clocked a new world record.

Nordqvist, Christian. "What is Serotonin? What Does Serotonin Do?" http://www.medicalnewstoday.com, accessed August 2011.

Official FINA website: http://www/fina.org, accessed March 23, 2013.

"Opiate Addiction Opiate Rapid Detox Opiates." http://opiates.org, accessed

September 26, 2011. Information about the effects of opiates on brain and on naturally occurring endorphins and their relationship to pain management.

Otto, Michael W., and Jasper A. J. Smits. *Exercise for Mood and Anxiety: Proven Strategies for Overcoming Depression and Enhancing Well-being.* New York: Oxford University Press, 2011.

"Peirsol Defends Title," *Daily Pilot,* March 11, 2007.

Powers, Pauline, MD, and Ron Thompson, MD. *The Exercise Balance: What's Too Much, What's Too Little, and What's Just Right for You.* Carlsbad, Californa: Gürze Books, 2008.

Ratey, John J., and Eric Hagerman. *Spark: The Revolutionary New Science of Exercise and the Brain.* New York: Little, Brown, 2008.

Redfin. http://www.redfin.com/CA/Costa-Mesa/957-Magellan-St-92626/home/3710298, accessed October 2011.

Reynolds, Gretchen. "Prescribing Exercise to Treat Depression." *New York Times* Well blog. August 31, 2011. http://well.blogs.nytimes.com/2011/08/31/prescribing-exercise-to-treat-depression/.

"Sammy Lee." USA Diver: http://www.usadiver.com/who_is/Who_is_Sammy_lee2htm, accessed December 2010.

Saslow, Eli. "Siblings Swimming Toward the Olympics," *Washington Post.* August 3, 2006.

Schneider, Terri. *Triathlon Revolution: Training, Technique, and Inspiration.* Seattle, WA: Mountaineers Books, 2008.

"Serotonin" entry on *Wikipedia.* http://en.wikipedia.org/wiki/Serotonin, accessed August 2011.

Shaver, Brent. "Local Siblings' Rivalry the Best Kind at Meet," *Orange County Register,* August 10, 2006.

Shenk, David. *The Genius in All of Us: Why Everything You've Been Told about Genetics, Talent, and IQ Is Wrong.* New York: Doubleday, 2010.

"SSRI use for anxiety and depression," Mayo Clinic website. http://www.mayoclinic.com/health/generalize-anxiety-disorder/DS00502/DSECTION=lifestyle%2Dand%2Dhome%2Drememdies and http://www.mayoclinic.com/health/ssris/MH00066, accessed October 2012.

"Sunkist Growers, Incorporated." http://www.sunkist.com, accessed March 2013.

"Sunkist" entry on *Wikipedia.* http://en.wikipedia.org/wiki/Sunkist_Growers,_Incorporated, accessed March 2013.

"Swimming—Aaron Peirsol Bodysurfing Video," by GoSwim. YouTube.

Uploaded January 7, 2009. http://www.youtube.com/watch?v=rtMwtX-rkLHM, accessed January 2011.

Sydney Olympic Park Aquatic Centre website. http://www.aquaticcentre.com.au/, accessed September 2011.

"Sydney Olympic Aquatic Center" entry on *Wikipedia*. http://en.wikipedia.org/wiki/Sydney_International_Aquatic_Centre, accessed September 2011.

Trivedi, M. H., T. L. Greer, S. N. Blair, T. S. Church, T. J. Carmody, B. D. Grannemann, D. I. Galper, A. L. Dunn, C. P. Earnest, P. Sunderajan, and S. S. Henley. "Exercise as an Augmentation Treatment for Non-remitted Major Depressive Disorder: A Randomized, Parallel Dose Comparison." *Journal of Clinical Psychiatry* 72 (5) (2011): 677-84.

University of Texas Athletics official website. http://www.texassports.com, accessed November 2011.

USA Swimming. http://www.USASwimming.org, accessed May 2010 through March 2013.

Virgen, Steve. "Peirsol Renews Passion in Triathlon." *Daily Pilot*. September 2008.

"Wella Peirsol Hartig: Mom of Two Olympic-Level Athletes Advises Parents Not to Pressure Kids to Succeed in Sports." http://www.MomsTeam.com, and http://www.momsteam.com/blog/may-sports-moms-month/wella-peirsol-hartig-being-mom-2-olympic-athletes-says-no-pressure-on-kids-to-succeed#ixzz2OPGOlm00, accessed May 2012.

Weir, Kirsten. "The Exercise Effect." American Psychological Association. http://www.apa.org/monitor/2011/12/exercise.aspx, accessed December 20, 2011.

Williams, Venus, and Kelly E. Carter. *Come to Win: Business Leaders, Artists, Doctors, and Other Visionaries on How Sports Can Help You Top Your Profession*. New York: Amistad, an Imprint of Harper Collins, 2010.

Winzer, Ingo. "Back to Basics." *Mortgage Banking*, Mortgage Bankers Association newsletter. October 2000.

Wooden, John, and Steve Jamison. *My Personal Best: Life Lessons from an All-American Journey*. New York: McGraw-Hill, 2004.

"World record progression 200 metres backstroke" entry on *Wikipedia*. http://en.wikipedia.org/wiki/World_record_progression_200_metres_backstroke, accessed January 2013.

Young, Simon N. "How to Increase Serotonin in the Human Brain without Drugs," *Journal of Psychiatry & Neuroscience*, November 2007, 32 (6):

394-399. http://www.ncbi.nim.nih.gov/pmc/articles/PMC2077351, accessed February 2013.

NON-PUBLISHED SOURCES

Copies of original court documents, as noted in endnotes, acquired October 2012.

Scanned yearbook pages relating to Bena Boltin Wells, acquired March 2012.

Verification of Orange County business card details, badges, and information about welfare office particulars for 1993–1994. Phone conversations and e-mails, April 6–7, 2011.

Family archives of photographs, newspaper clippings, scrapbooks belonging to Wella and Tim Hartig, Hayley Peirsol, and Aaron Peirsol.

About the Authors

WELLA HARTIG is a retired swim mom who wanted to share her story. Although her struggles are not unique, she hopes to inspire other parents to "dream big" (as Aaron often says) for their children—regardless of economic circumstances or seeming lack of opportunities. She and her husband Tim now have time to enjoy surfing and tropical breezes. Wella has started a line of clothing and volunteers at the local library. The two of them still run and swim every day.

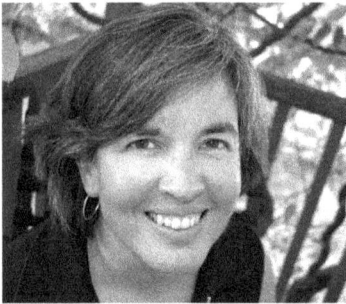

LAURA COTTAM SAJBEL is drawn to the rich and colorful narratives of individuals sharing stories we need to know. She has turned those stories into articles, poetry, and fiction for more than twenty years. Starting her career in magazines, she earned a master's degree in writing from the University of Southern California, then taught creative writing and literature at Loyola Marymount University and at El Camino College. She served on the Author Selection Committee at the start of the Texas Book Festival and has run Young Writers' Workshops for the neighborhood elementary in Austin. The mother of three athletic children and wife of a cyclist, Laura swims, kayaks, and is certified to scuba dive.

www.ingramcontent.com/pod-product-compliance
Lightning Source LLC
Chambersburg PA
CBHW030932090426
42737CB00007B/398